GOD ALWAYS WINS

And You Always Win In God

By Ella C. Brunt

A true Life story of
CODY BRUNT
Our "MIRACLE IN MOTION"

America Star Books

Second printing 2014

America Star Books has allowed this work to remain exactly as the author intended, verbatim, without editorial input.

Cover design: Ben Williams

Hardcover 9781632498434
Softcover 1588510689
PUBLISHED BY AMERICA STAR BOOKS, LLLP
www.americastarbooks.com
Baltimore

Printed in the United States of America

Special Thanks...

To the Lord Jesus Christ, Who alone could have brought us through this tragedy into triumph? All glory and honor is His!

To my husband, Ted, who has been a 'rock' and a steady hand to help and encourage me throughout Cody's recovery. He has spent many hours helping me with this manuscript.

To James Benson, who encouraged me to chronicle this miracle. He was such a blessing and stood with us many hours at the hospital, witnessing God's power in action.

To Kenneth Copeland for the revelation that *"Faith-filled words dominate the laws of death."*

To Jerry Savelle for the teaching on *"The Established Heart"* in Psalm 112.

To Virdeen Munoz for her fantastic editing talents.

To Darryl Hicks, whose suggestions, experience, and expertise added to the adventure of this project.

To the countless friends and Believers who prayed with us to see Cody's total recovery.

CONTENTS

Introduction

God still works miracles each and every day, and Cody Brunt is living proof. As a wife and mother, I will be forever changed after experiencing the miraculous restoration of the life seen in my son, Cody. As we endured those seemingly endless days in the hospitals, my heart went out to other parents around us. Many of them were in much the same hopeless circumstances as we were. I hurt for them in their distress because inasmuch as our situations were similar, the forces we all depended on to rectify our problems were very different. In too many cases, the parents were often ignorant of God's Word; His loving, healing nature, and His miracle-working power.

> *"My people are destroyed for lack of knowledge."*
> *Hosea 4:6*

Days passed when my only focus was a scripture providing light in a dark place. *Finding* my miracle answer in the Bible meant *having* my miracle answer in the natural. The Word of God was my source of strength during the days when Cody was kept alive by life support systems. I used that time to re-read and concentrate on the miracles of Jesus, knowing that if Jesus did it in the Bible, He would do it for me. In Luke 7:11-17, Jesus raised a widow's only son back to life, during the boy's funeral. In John 11:1-46, Jesus called his friend Lazarus back to life, after 4 days in the grave. In Luke 8:49-56, Jesus restored life to the daughter of Jairus, after being thought "too late" to do any good. Jesus was never "too late" to work God's Will and that was exactly the kind of miracle-working power we needed.

We knew God's will for Cody was a long, strong, healthy life, and we knew God's Word would work for us, just like it had in the scripture Psalm 118:17 *"I shall not die, but live and declare the works of the Lord."*

We were put in a place where our faith was on display.

As we watched our small son, in that sterile hospital bed attached to life support systems, the doctors gave us the report of irreversible brain damage and the prognosis of little hope. In this darkest of all situations for a parent, we clung to our faith, believing God *could* and *would* do the 'impossible' for us. Our confession over our son was just the opposite of the medical reports and we took every opportunity to say it.

The words that we speak can bring either death or life (Proverbs 18:21). Words are a creative force (Isaiah 57:19), and we are the product of words that we have spoken over ourselves (Matthew 12:35-37). God used His Words to create the universe. We spoke God's Word over Cody's life and trusted God to do what the doctors could not do. We are God's creation and He has no favorites. What God did for us, in bringing our son back to life and health, is available to anyone who will believe for it. Jesus purchased everything we will ever need on the cross.

"So shall my word be that goeth forth out of my mouth: it shall not return unto me void, but it shall accomplish that which I please, and it shall prosper in the thing whereto I sent it."

Isaiah 55:11

The power that God has placed in a spoken word is not the subject of this book. The truth of that power is, however, a valuable lesson to be gleaned from this story. We spoke

God's Word over Cody's life from the beginning and we have watched that Word change the darkest of circumstances. Jesus did all the work for us. He laid all the foundations and paid all the prices. Just receive it.

May this book build hope and faith in you to believe the reality of the Word of God and to appropriate its power for your situations, no matter how impossible they may seem to you. **God always wins, and you always win in God!**

Chapter 1

Just Find Him!

The gulf breeze seemed to fan the excitement that was building around the ball field. The tall stadium lights added a unique but appropriate iridescence. The t-ball season's grand finale all-star game was about to begin. My husband Ted and I were perched in the stands, like all the other proud parents, to cheer on our "stars'. Our nine-year old daughter, Brittany, was sitting next to Grammy (Ted's mother) and we were excited for the game to begin. Parents filled the stands with their cameras ready; video cameras were mounted and rolling. There was great anticipation for the umpire to announce, "Play Ball!"

Even though the sky was clear and full of stars, shining brightly overhead, our focus was on the field as our seven-year old son took his position at third base. As exciting as this contest was for all the young athletes and their supporters, Cody's participation had an added dimension. Ten months prior to this event, our Cody was dead.

Wednesday, July 2, 1997

The morning had started leisurely. The kids were sleeping late and Ted had just left for work. I took advantage of the quiet time by settling in at the serene place on the couch. My haven for a few moments of devotion and Bible study time was vital to starting each day right.

Both Brittany and Cody had been involved in the summer track program. Today was a field event meet, so we sat this one out. We weren't rushed to get to the track by 7:30 this morning to work out. After the kids awoke, we loaded the car with snacks and munchies and drove across town to check on the progress of the new home that we were building. As I drove through the gate and under the big sixty year old oak trees that lined the future driveway, I couldn't help but think how the goodness of God had led us to this point in our lives.

Since the children didn't share my enthusiasm for the sound of saws and hammers and the aroma of freshly cut lumber, they bored quickly with the activity of the work site. Brittany and Cody were anticipating the sailing date we had with my brother Ed's youngest son, Wallace, later that afternoon. The last thing Ted told me that morning was to pick up the kid's life jackets. On the way out of town, we stopped by the home of our friends, Roland and Linda Kelley, to do just that. Also, Cody had to stop by Wendy's to get an order of chicken nuggets for a snack "on the road' to Clear Lake, to meet Wallace. The morning had been so warm and peaceful, quite literally the calm before the storm.

As we drove onto the parking lot at Clear Lake, we noticed that Wallace had arrived before us and already had the boat in the water, tied up at the pier area. He was getting the ice chest in the boat and was almost ready to go. There were several wave runners (jet skiers) enjoying the hot (mid 90-degree weather), clear summer day. Several people were loading and launching boats from the dock area. This was to be our first sailboat ride. I carefully put the life jackets on Cody, then on Brittany. We were excited to get out on the water and feel the wind at our backs driving us across the lake.

It was windy and, even though Wallace was an experienced sailboat operator, he was having trouble getting underway. A friendly boater (who was introduced later as Dan Darnell) asked if we would like to be towed out away from the launch area. I made a comment about the unusual style of his boat.

It had a center console, but the front bow of the boat had a flat platform area. It just hit me as a little unusual. The boater explained that he was testing the boat out, since it had been in the shop for repairs. They were taking the boat on vacation the next day. We took him up on his offer and got a tow about fifty yards from the dock area. Wallace put up the main sail and was preparing the jib in the front of the boat. Cody and Brittany were told to get in the covered area in the front of the boat, out of the way of the main sail, until things were ready. My brother Ed, his wife Carolyn, and Carolyn's mother, Geneva, had just arrived and were walking up to the pier area. We waved to them. Now we had an audience!

The last jib was being set in place when the boat leaned to the right and kept on leaning. Wallace, who was in the front of the boat, reached down and lifted Brittany to me. Cody was on the right side of the boat, but the sail was dividing us. Neither Wallace nor I could reach him. Cody was reaching for me, his eyes wide in terror. Things happened so fast, yet it seemed in slow motion. I didn't even have time to comfort him with, "It's O.K., Cody. Just swim out." I was less than ten feet away from my son, but couldn't touch him. He had taken private swimming lessons the previous summer and I was confident of his ability to recover in the water. The boat silently continued listing to the right. Soon the boat was on its side and Cody was out of sight.

We waited for Cody to swim out, but he never came up. We kept watching, expecting that cherubic, tan little face to pop up from the water. The moments marched on and the realization of a problem hit me with a force I've never known, before or since. It was unforeseen, unexpected, and powerfully gripping. Brittany and I clung to one another. Wallace dove under the boat. He came up without Cody. He dove again and again. My son was still under the water. I explained to Brittany that Cody was in trouble and asked her to pray in the Spirit. The Holy Spirit prays the perfect will of God every time. According to Romans 8:*26 "Likewise the Spirit also helpeth our infirmities: for we know not what we should pray for as we ought: but the Spirit itself (Himself) maketh intercession for us with groanings which cannot be uttered."* I didn't even think to turn to the dock and ask Ed to call for help. In fact, they were unaware anything was wrong. I felt numb. By this time, the natural response of a mother whose son is missing under the water would be to scream and demonstrate any number of degrees of panic. That could have been my reaction, but I felt a deep, inner calm, which seemed to take control. It was the presence of God, and I wanted desperately to cooperate with Him.

Wallace was doing everything he could to locate and rescue Cody. My only thought was to call out to Jesus, so I did just that. Shouting out loud, "***J-E-S-U-S!***" several times. I was reminded of blind Bartemaus in the Bible. One day he was sitting by the roadside and Jesus walked by. In his desperation he called out, *"Jesus, Son of David, have mercy on me!"* It worked for him and I was just as desperate. Just like Bartemaus had done almost 2000 years ago, I called out, "Jesus, Son of David, have mercy on me! Jesus, have mercy on us!" Wallace came up and shouted, "NOOOOOO!" I didn't realize that Wallace had been locating Cody during these rescue attempts, but was unable to free him from the rigging. When Wallace first found Cody under the boat, he was kicking and fighting to get loose. Each time Wallace pulled, trying to free him. One last time Wallace returned for Cody, but this time Cody's body was lifeless and still. Wallace was visibly frustrated, so I called to him and encouraged him to keep trying. The thought occurred to me that if we lost Cody, we would lose Wallace as well. Several years earlier Wallace was diagnosed with "bipolar manic depression." In my heart I knew if Cody didn't make it, the guilt and responsibility of a tragic outcome would surely demolish Wallace's life. We just *had* to come through this somehow. The devil was *not* going to destroy our family.

Time seemed to stand still. Everything else disappeared and there was only a sailboat that refused to release my son. My next thought was a casket holding Cody's small body. The vision of Ted and I walking along with only Brittany startled me. I shook that picture out of my mind and spoke to its author. ***"NO!" "No devil, you are not going to take any more of my babies!"*** (Both our children had miracle births to begin with. Ted and I had physical complications even to become pregnant. God supernaturally healed our bodies to conceive children. We had lost our first child to miscarriage and I knew the heartbreak of losing a child and was determined not to allow Satan to steal any more.)

The Bible gives a good measuring stick in John 10:10 "The thief (Satan) cometh not but for to steal, and to kill, and to destroy: I am come that they might have life and have it more abundantly." recognized that the author of this accident was not God, but the devil. I was not going to settle for that scenario. I had a CHOICE to make. Either let my emotions take over and panic or stay calm and allow my inner man to take over and control the situation. I made the choice. My mind turned off and my spirit deep within me took over. I had no fear, just a perfect peace, "the peace that passes all understanding", (Philippians 4:7), engulfed me. I allowed the Spirit of God to pray and intercede through me. I realized that too much time had passed, my son was dead. Comforted in knowing that God is in the resurrection business and that He would surely do it for us, we kept searching for Cody's body. A woman jet skier came along side of us and asked if we needed assistance. After I quickly told her of our situation, she went to get help and took Brittany back to the dock as a passenger on her Jet Ski. Before I released her, I instructed Brittany to stay with Aunt Carolyn and told her that everything was going to be all right. I began to dive for Cody and pray against brain damage, disability, or handicaps, knowing God would raise him from the dead, and I expected a complete recovery. My prayer included the request that all medical attention given to Cody would **only do him good and no harm.** I stood against death…I said aloud, "Cody will LIVE and not DIE and declare the works of the Lord!" according to Psalm 118:17.

At that moment, the words of our pastor resounded in my mind:

"What happens next is determined by what happens now."

That word was so supportive. Addressing the devil, my words were "Cody belongs to God and not to you, Satan! The blood of Jesus is against you!" Then I asked God to help us locate my son. We continued to dive in the dark, dirty water. "Oh God, You can raise him up, just help us find him!"

Wallace kept diving in and trying to free Cody. The ropes and rigging had entangled Cody's life jacket, attaching him to the boat. I continued diving until I touched something. I came up, pulling it with me, but it was a blue cover. It was the case Wallace used earlier for storing the sails. I threw it aside and then I can't remember much more.

After some period of time, I looked over and saw Wallace come up with Cody's limp, blue body. The last time Wallace dove in, Cody broke loose easily, pulling free from the tangle of ropes. The previous rescues had proved futile, Cody had been firmly entangled and didn't budge.

Days later, at the hospital, Greg Pikar, a young man on a Jet Ski, told us how he arrived on the scene as Wallace was pulling Cody up to the water's surface. At that time we asked him if anyone had helped Wallace up to that point. Greg said there was no one else in the water at that time. To me, the only way to explain that event is to say we had the **"fourth man"** of the fiery furnace in Clear Lake that afternoon to release Cody from the ropes that attached him under the boat!

During this time, the jet skier delivered Brittany to Carolyn at the docks. She reported to Carolyn and Ed, "Cody is hurt, call 911!" They didn't understand what she meant by "hurt". They couldn't see clearly from the view they had. They knew the kids had on their life jackets. What could she mean?

Ed went to his car to use the cell phone and make the call. Carolyn left Brittany with Geneva and went for help. There were two jet skiers that had just loaded their crafts onto their trailer. Carolyn ran over to these men and asked if they would go help. (These were two off duty Houston police officers, Bob Opperman and John McGowan.) There wasn't enough time to unload the trailer, so Bob caught a ride with the jet skier who had brought Brittany back to the dock.

Bob tried three times to mount the craft, it would go a little ways and tilt over. The craft was too small for both riders. Carolyn prayed as they continued on their way to help us. The fourth time worked and they were on their way out to the boat. Carolyn went back to where Geneva and Brittany were standing. The three kept praying while they watched. Ed came back from the car and could only imagine the scenario being played out only a short distance away.

Just as the two jet skiers reached the scene, Wallace was bringing Cody out of the water. Bob helped to completely free Cody from the rigging. As Cody's lifeless body was lifted up to the jet skier, it bent backward 90 degrees. I knew he was dead. Even though I saw the awkward position and the unmistakable blue color, there was an intense assurance that everything would be all right. We now had a body for the Lord to raise up! As this effort was being made, to return to shore, the Jet Ski malfunctioned. It would not start. The blue sail-case I had found earlier and thrown aside had gotten in the engine and stalled it out. However, all was not lost. About that time, the boat that had towed us out earlier returned and offered assistance. This boat (that I had thought odd-shaped) proved to be **just what we needed**. The flat bow was a perfect platform to perform CPR. The stalled Jet Ski proved to be a blessing, the *boat* was what we needed. They lifted Cody's body from the Jet Ski to the boat. Wallace and Bob pulled up and boarded the boat. They checked Cody out. He had no pulse and was not breathing. CPR was immediately given to Cody. Cody was most certainly dead. I was still in the water when they first administered CPR. As they began to resuscitate him, a gush of water and food exploded from Cody's mouth. *The recovery was on!* I shouted at the driver to not leave me. I quickly swam to the boat and, with no ladder, miraculously boarded and kept repeating, *"I speak life into Cody. I speak life into Cody!"*

Officer Bob and Wallace continued to work on Cody as we headed for the dock. When we reached it, they carefully lifted Cody's body to a crowd of people that had now gathered to help. As I watched, I thought it was strange that Cody's life jacket was down around his knees. It wasn't until later that I was informed the ropes had entangled the life jacket, which was what held him under.

The paramedics hadn't arrived yet. My attention focused on Cody's chest and a purple bruise that wasn't there when we started this outing. It looked like the imprint of the T-Rex on his necklace. It must have made a mark as they pushed on his chest to get his lungs and heart working. I told one of the rescuers to "be careful and stop pushing on him if he starts breathing". Was he breathing yet? At first, the paramedics were dispatched to a nearby harbor. When they couldn't see any activity, they drove down the street to where we were. The EMS team was from the fire station based at NASA. As soon as they arrived, they immediately started working on Cody. I kept praying and speaking "life" into him. I looked across the way to the pier area and saw Brittany with Carolyn, waiting together and praying. They seemed so close, yet so far away. I saw everything around us in bits and pieces, all the while watching for Cody to take a breath. Now the emergency team was using a bag mask resuscitator on Cody. They seemed to know what they were doing.

By now many people had gathered around us. Ed came out on the dock to console his son, while watching for signs of life in Cody. Wallace was exhausted, slumped against a piling with his legs dangling over the side of the pier. The paramedics administered oxygen to Wallace and treated him for shock. Not only was there activity on the dock area but now I heard sounds in the sky. Several helicopters from Houston television stations were now circling over head. It annoyed me a little as they hovered over like vultures wanting a news story. The paramedics had taken over the CPR on Cody and I felt a little in the way. At this point, I knew I couldn't do anything to assist them. I went to the car to get my mobile phone to contact Ted, who would be on his way home from work by this time. He did not answer the phone, so I had to leave a brief message on the phone recorder. What a message to have to leave your spouse. I knew I'd have to word it carefully.

Things were happening real fast now. John (the other off-duty police officer that had been loading the Jet Skies on the trailer at the launch area) was in the parking lot telling people to move their cars to make room for a medical helicopter to land. I was re-parking my car and leaving Ted the message at the same time. The Life Flight helicopter was landing. I got word that they would be transporting Cody to Hermann Hospital in Houston. My message to Ted was brief, but enough to let him know that there had been an accident and that Cody had been under the water for a while. I concluded the message for Ted to meet us at the hospital. I returned to the dock, where they were continuing to work on Cody. One of the paramedics standing guard at the entrance of the dock looked up at me and commented, "Are you still praying?" All I could reply was, ***"Lady, that is all I can do!"***

The Life Flight helicopter had been in close proximity, returning from transferring a patient to a Galveston hospital, when they received the call. I was not allowed to accompany Cody on the flight to Houston. We had to make other plans now.

As the chopper lifted off the parking lot, I made another call, this time to my pastor. Miraculously, he answered the phone at his home. I remained calm and began with…

"No weapon formed against Cody will prosper…"

After hearing the situation, he prayed with us for Cody's full recovery. As he continued praying, some investigating officers were coming to the car window and asking me for more information…Pastor concluded the prayer and told me, ***"This is not unto death. Cody will recover."*** I was filled with peace and supernatural strength!

As I walked back to the dock area, I became anxious to get to the hospital. Plans were being changed to bring Wallace by ambulance to Hermann instead of a near-by hospital in Clear Lake. Wallace was loaded into an ambulance and grasped his mother's hand and whispered, "Cody just *has* to be alright." Carolyn knew that Wallace would not be 'all right' until Cody was 'all right'. Carolyn was going to ride in the ambulance with Wallace. My brother, Ed, checked on his son and informed me of the change of plans.

Ed insisted on driving me to the hospital. It was rush-hour traffic, as businesses were releasing their workers at the end of the day. I told Ed I could handle the drive into Houston myself, but Big Brother insisted *he* would be driving. We all got in my car and were finally on our way to Houston. Brittany and Geneva were in the back seat, Ed and I in front. The traffic was congested as far as we could see. We spent the time singing praise choruses and praying, in between my phone calls requesting prayer from friends. At this point, I knew I needed reinforcements. The first call was to my friend, Misty May, at her business. I asked her to please call Chris Stefan, a neighbor by our new house sight. I needed her to keep an eye out for Ted in case he went to the lot first and to give him the message. I called several other friends to have them start praying. With each call I would start out, *"No weapon formed against Cody will prosper…"*. **I knew what we said would be life or death to our son**.

Our words at this point were life or death to our son (Proverbs18:21) and we were choosing God's words of life.

During the drive, Brittany fell asleep. We finally made it to the hospital…with no help from the traffic.

Chapter 2

GOD GAVE US A PLAN

Ted went straight to the apartment from work. He said later, that when he touched the front door knob that afternoon, he felt that something was wrong. My husband is not one to talk on the phone and it was very out of character for him to check the answering machine, but that day he did. He listened to message #1. It was one of my friends and she wanted me to return her call. Message #2 was mine from the dock at Clear Lake. He listened, rewound it, and listened again. Could what he was hearing be true? His first reaction was simply unbelief, but the noise of the helicopter in the background made it all too real. He immediately called his mom (Grammy) and asked her to listen. She had just been watching the 5 o-clock news. She said the television station had just shown the dock scene and reported that a little girl had drowned. Ted assured her that it was Cody and asked her to ride to Houston with him. He picked her up in his truck and headed off to the hospital. They prayed all the way, and arrived at the hospital before us, even though they came from Texas City, 35 miles away.

At the hospital...

Ed dropped me off at the emergency room entrance, then parked the car. Still in my bathing suit and water shoes, I asked for my son. Finding Ted at the admitting desk, I threw my arms around him and held on tight. Ted had already talked to Carolyn and was filled in on what was happening. Ted was 'pumped up' in the Spirit and had already given Carolyn and the emergency room admitting clerk a sermon. He proclaimed to them that God was going to restore Cody 100 percent and that Cody would *walk* out of that hospital healed and whole. He was not going to compromise his confession.

Ted was very emphatic about what our plan would be. He had heard from God. As he and his mother were praying and driving to the hospital, God spoke to him twice about the situation reminding him of phrases heard in sermons from years past:

"Faith-filled words dominate the laws of death" and "Bad news don't shake him".

These were His words of encouragement.

Ted proceeded to present me with our strategy to see Cody through this demonic attack. Our plan was to:

- **Speak only faith-filled words and the desired end result. Cody will *walk* out of Hermann Hospital 100 per cent *healed* and *whole.***
- **Do not allow one word of doubt or unbelief to come out of our mouths—*not one. If we can't speak the Word, don't speak.***
- **Do not allow *anyone* who cannot speak faith-filled words, or the desired end result, around Cody.**

Soon, a doctor from the emergency room came out and gave us a brief report. I remember him saying gravely, "Cody is a very sick little boy…he is a near-drowning victim." I asked what that term meant, because I had seen my son actually drown. What did he mean by *"near drowning"*? He answered, *"The only difference between your son and a drowning victim is that a drowning victim is dead."*

Time stood still for a few seconds after his report. He continued to say Cody's lungs were very congested and hemorrhaging from the salt water. They could not stop the bleeding and if it continued, there was an experimental drug that they could try. He emphatically said that *they knew* Cody had brain damage and they expected his brain to begin swelling within 24 hours. They would use a procedure to drill holes in his skull and release the pressure. He predicted that Cody would be fighting pneumonia, because of the salt water and contamination in his lungs.

The doctor asked for our permission to begin special high-powered antibiotics to help prevent the infection from increasing. At this time, Cody was being kept alive by life support systems. He said the next few hours were critical, *if* Cody made it through. For now, they just wanted to stabilize his condition and see if he could make it through the night.

> **We heard with our ears what the doctors were saying, but it wasn't sinking into our hearts.**

Ted and I listened intently. We heard with our ears what the doctor was saying, but it wasn't sinking into our hearts. Ted told the doctor that we were Christians and believed that God was going to raise our son up to perfect health. All we wanted to do was see our son and pray for him. I'm sure they thought we were in **'denial'**. We were.

We denied the right for those symptoms to stay in our son.

Jesus went to the cross and bore our sicknesses and diseases. We knew we were redeemed from every curse of the law according to Galatians 3:13. The doctors and staff at Hermann Hospital were so compassionate and skillful. Several of our friends made the comment that we were in the best hospital for the injuries Cody had sustained. We understood that doctors report <u>facts</u>. We were declaring that **FAITH overrides the facts!**

While they continued to stabilize Cody, we were escorted into a private area of the Life Flight waiting room. Great care was taken to guard our privacy. Three television cameramen were already at the emergency room entrance when Carolyn and Wallace arrived at the hospital. News media were perched and ready for a story. The hospital personnel diligently shielded us from the news teams.

During the waiting time, friends started arriving and encouraging us. Ed's eldest son, Edmund, and his wife, Tina, H.D. and Katherine Reddin (friends from Baytown), and Roland and Linda Kelley were there. It was a small room and we filled every seat. Ted explained our victory plan to everyone, *"Only speak words of faith. Don't speak any negative words or words of doubt. If you can't speak words of faith, please wait outside!"* After Ted's announcement, we did not repeat the accident details again, only the expected end result. It was important not to keep repeating the details of the accident. We **guarded our hearts** and minds, looking at the expected end results of our faith.

> It was important not to keep repeating the details of the accident.

As a mother, I longed to see Cody. Oh, how I wanted to see him and hold him again. Wallace was being treated in the emergency room down the hall. They were treating him for a puncture wound in his upper thigh and doing some chest x-rays. He had taken some water in his lungs as well. Wallace was asking to see Brittany, but the halls were crawling with reporters looking for the story and his requests were denied.

The incident was mentally taking a toll on him and he wanted to make sure his little niece was ok. We were so proud of Wallace for staying with the rescue and finding Cody. I had stepped out of the room to get a drink of water and look for Ted. As soon as I opened the door, I saw a friend from church, Rick Herzog. He was talking with Ted. Rick and his family had arrived at the Wednesday night church service and were told of the accident. They immediately left church and came to Houston to be with us. The display of love and concern from these friends spoke volumes. guess all the emotions I had bottled up inside until this point burst out. I began to cry for the first time. In my heart I knew everything was going to be all right, but so much had happened in the last few hours that my mind was overloaded. Was this really happening or was I going to wake up and find it was all a dream? The staff was so helpful, they found Brittany some shoes and me a pair of scrubs to wear. We were both in our bathing suits, with shirt cover-ups. I had on water shoes, but Brittany was barefooted. Our attire gave away our identity, so we needed a disguise.

A staff person came in after what seemed an eternity, but was actually 60-90 minutes later. She explained to us that the doctors were getting ready to take Cody up to PICU Children's Hospital. She proceeded to escort us upstairs to see Cody in the Pediatric Intensive Care Unit (PICU). Almost simultaneously, Wallace was in the process of being released from the hospital and Ed and Carolyn were down the hall facilitating that. Our procession left the Life Flight waiting area and traveled up the elevator to the third floor. As we turned down a hall, I glanced up and saw a large group of people standing together. As I took a closer look, I recognized them as church friends, waiting just outside the PICU doors. At the time, I did not know that my nurse-friend, Misty May, had stood in as 'my sister' and all the friends were 'family' in order for the doctors to release information to them. Misty is a registered nurse and knew all the right questions to ask. Misty had asked the doctor if Cody had a pain reflex. He said, "No". She asked if he had a deep pain reflex. Again, he said, "No". She asked about the oxygen level (PO2) in his lungs. Hours after the accident it was only 40 percent. A normal level is 98-99 percent. She understood very well how serious Cody's condition was. She relayed the report to the waiting friends and they were already praying. They knew Cody's condition better than we did at the time and knew how and what to pray for. Ted and I were ushered in to see our son for the first time. There was such a peace and grace present that words cannot adequately explain. God knew of my tendency to faint at needles and medical paraphernalia, but the Lord sustained me as my eyes surveyed the area. Our son's little tan body lay motionless on those white sheets. Cody had so many tubes and stuff on him. I'd never seen such a small person have so much medical apparatus on them. The life support system was working to keep him alive. The head physician in PICU, Dr. Ralph Frate, stepped up and gave us his report. It was the same report we heard downstairs.

The doctor's report was grim, but our trust was in the report of the Lord.

His statistics, according to the medical records, were:

I.   Very ill
II. Respiration: 100 percent saturated, RR=22
III. Extremities: cold
IV. Color: bluish-gray
V.   Loose incisor

VI. X-rays of lungs show total "white out'

Ted listened politely, thanked him for his report, and then asked him to listen to *"God's Report"*. The Bible says in Isaiah 53:1 ***"Who hath believed our report? And to whom is the arm of the Lord revealed?"*** Ted began to tell him that we were "believers in the Lord Jesus Christ' and all we wanted to do was to lay hands on Cody according to Mark 16:18. The doctor asked, "Oh, what Christian sect are you with?" Ted thought for a couple of seconds and replied, ***"We just believe that Jesus Christ is Lord to the glory of God the Father."*** Ted knew that this was not the proper time to teach about how ***God has given Jesus a Name that is above every name that is named*** (Philippians 2:9,10) *including brain damage, aspiration, and pneumonia.*

Ted asked if the friends we had outside could come into pray for Cody. Dr. Frate told us, "Bring them in." I asked "All of them?" He said, "Sure." That evening, H.D. and Katherine Reddin, Roland and Linda Kelley, Don and Shirley Stidham, Cheryl Martin, and Ted and I proceeded into PICU with a mission. Grammy (Ted's mom), Edmund and Tina, (Ed, Carolyn and Wallace somehow got disconnected from the group) Misty May, Rick, Ricky and Tina Herzog, and James and Debbie Benson were also there with us. (Shirley decided to stay out and watch the two children. Along with Ricky Herzog and Brittany, they remained in the waiting room.) The group went in, circled around the bed, prayed, and laid hands on Cody. If they could not get close enough to touch Cody, they laid hands on a nurse, doctor, or anyone else close. Ted asked our church care minister, James Benson, to lead in prayer.

Tubes, NG lines, ventilator, just about every machine that could be utilized, were hooked up to Cody's little body. One of the first things I noticed was blood on his lip. It wasn't there at the dock. We learned later that when a person is intubated, time is of the essence and the metal instrument used in the procedure had knocked loose three teeth.

I looked at Cody's oxygen level and, at that time, it registered 40. Later, I learned that was an indication of definite, irreversible brain damage. As I viewed the area, I saw Cody's name and the doctor's name on a paper at the head of the bed. I asked Ted to get a pen and write some scriptures on the paper. In Habakkuk 2:2, the Bible says to *"write the vision and make it plain"*; and to *"write the scriptures over the door posts"* (Deuteronomy 6:9). This was as close as we could get for the moment.

After our prayer time, the medical staff asked for our permission to perform some additional medical procedures. We had to leave the room for them to continue to treat our son. The hospital was very gracious to give us a room directly across the hall from the PICU doors. The group of friends all prayed together again, before leaving for the night. As the first group of people was leaving, others were arriving after church that evening. In that group were Michael Hallam, Cody's principal, R.C. Colbert, Joe Ramirez, one of my former students and his mother and sister. Others, too, came that evening, but I only saw them visually. I wasn't talking to people since my mind was focused on Cody in the room across the hall.

Roland and Linda helped us make a list of things they would pick up at our apartment and bring back to us. They were preparing to take Brittany and Grammy home to Texas City. Before they left, we prayed over Brittany and believed that she would not be traumatized by the day's events—that the peace of God would overshadow her during this time of our separation. For the next few weeks, Brittany and Grammy were inseparable "buddies". I was still in a fog after all the afternoon's events. Any moment, I thought I'd wake up from this dream and things would be normal. As Misty was leaving the hospital, she asked me if she could do any thing for us. We so appreciated all she had done and just her being there was a great help. She paused and made a comment that would ring in my ears. "Now Ella, we don't want Cody to recover too quickly. We need the hospital to document this miracle." Being a little disoriented from the day's events and trying to stay focused, I had to really concentrate on what she had just said. Had I not understood where she was coming from, it would have been easy to take offense at that statement. Here my son is laying in the PICU and she's worried about documentation! If I had *my* way, Cody would have had his miracle on the dock and this entire hospital venture wouldn't have been necessary! Only God knew the timetable of events in the days to follow. It was not my time line, but His divine timing. Little did we know at the time just how long it would take to see our son recover. **Our faces were set; our mouths were only going to speak total recovery. We would not compromise our stand.**

Ed and Edmund went out and brought back drinks and hamburgers, since at this late hour the hospital cafeteria was closed. Ed insisted we needed to eat something to keep strong. I tried to eat, but food was the least of my desires at the time. During this intimate family time, Wallace and I tried to talk through the afternoon's events and reflect on just what had really happened out on the lake.

After taking Brittany and Grammy home, Roland and Linda went back to our apartment to gather the things we had listed. As Roland was gathering the things, he was impressed to bring back an 8x10 photograph of Cody. We had taken the photograph in March for his sixth birthday. They drove back to the hospital that same night, by this time it was early Thursday morning.

Ed, Carolyn, Edmund, and Tina left to drive back to Clear Lake and pick up their two vehicles at the boat launch parking lot. It was late. It had been a very stressful day and none of us realized the magnitude of all that would transpire in the next few weeks.

Cody's sixth year birthday photo, we placed it over his bed and confessed, "Cody will walk out of this hospital looking just like this!"

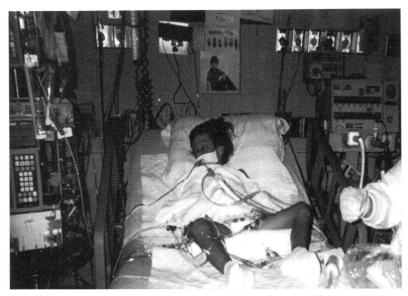

**Cody's life support apparatus IV pole on left, ventilator
on right.**

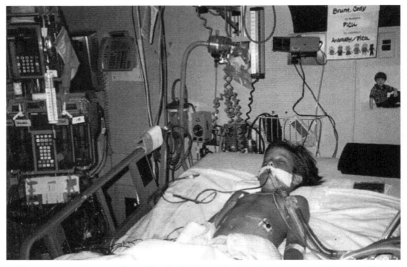

**Cassette player by Cody's head & picture on the wall—
focus point.**

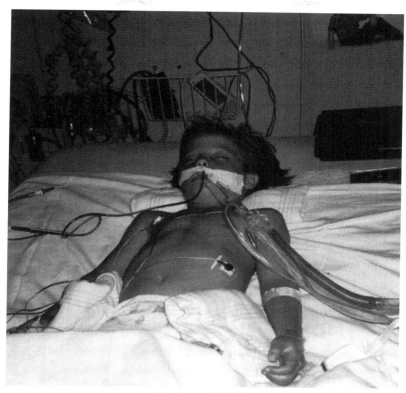

Cody in PICU

Chapter 3

Having Done All to Stand...Stand

> *"Cody will recover 100 percent and walk out of this hospital looking just like that picture!"*

Now the waiting and watching stage began. We were given a sleeping room for parents, down the hall from where Cody was. The first night was one of turmoil and sleeplessness. My heart felt like someone was ripping it out of my chest. There was an emotional, as well as spiritual, battle going on. In the natural, things looked so bleak, but in my heart I knew *"For with God, nothing shall be impossible."* (Luke 1:37) My head was battling with my spirit.

> **My mind kept trying to believe this was not really happening to us.**

Every time I'd close my eyes and try to rest, I'd have a flash back and see the terror in Cody's eyes, when he was reaching out to me as the boat tilted over and he went out of sight. My heart would grimace, as I put myself in his place and visualize the struggle he fought to get free from the ropes, only to get more entangled with every pull. What did he go through under the water? How did it feel to have water instead of air fill the lungs and suffocate in the darkness under the boat? My comfort was in knowing that God was under that boat with Cody and He was watching over him through it all. I quoted scriptures to myself and told the devil he could not torment me with those flashbacks. Cody was going to *"Live and not die and declare the works of the Lord!"* as stated in Psalm 118: 17.

Sleep evaded Ted and I. We could only toss and turn. The sleeping room we were given was cramped, with only a bunk bed and a small dresser. That's all there was to it; just a place to sleep. The bathroom facilities and shower were down the hall. There was no lamp or window. It was dark and isolated. The only light was that which crept through under the door. My mind kept trying to believe this was not really happening to us.

Even though Wallace was treated and released from the hospital, he wouldn't leave. He was given a bed in the waiting room across the hall from the PICU doors. I kept getting up and walking down the hall to ask the nurses if Cody's medical procedures were completed. The doctors were in the process of putting two catheters in Cody's upper legs. One was placed in Cody's left groin artery and one in his right groin vein to make it more accessible for medications and blood tests. It was a dangerous surgical procedure that required our signed permission for it to be performed. Each time I asked to see my son, the answer was the same; "The doctor is still working on Cody."

In the early hours of the morning, Ted and I were allowed to go see Cody. After seeing our son for the second time, the obstacles that were facing us seemed to be a huge mountain range. God was the only One who could come through for us.

When we got back to the room, I was impressed for Wallace, Ted, and I to take communion together. This would be an outward action to confirm our healing, blood covenant with Jesus. Sitting in the family waiting room, Ted, Wallace and I took communion. All we had was bread from a hamburger bun and Dr. Pepper to drink. Ted quoted the scriptures and we prayed together and partook of the elements.

> **We did everything we knew to do and relied on God to do what we could not do.**

We believed that with Jesus *and* the medical staff we would see our little boy recover 100 percent. I continually prayed that the medicines and treatments would do Cody only good and no harm. Sometime that morning, a nurse came in with Cody's Houston Astros tee shirt, shorts, and tennis shoes (the ones he was wearing at the time of the accident). She also had his necklace in a specimen jar. She commented, "I wanted you to be sure you get these." She was very professional and exact in her delivery. I felt odd receiving these, as though they were part of his "last rights' or something.

Cody was a big dinosaur admirer. He could name them all and tell you what they ate; meat or plants. We had bought him a silver T-Rex charm when he was about four years old and he wore it all the time on a chain around his neck. I noticed the chain was broken. They had obviously cut or broken the necklace when they were working on him in the helicopter or in the emergency room. In my heart, I believed that Cody would soon energetically wear this necklace, as well as play his "3-D Dinosaur" computer program again.

When we were allowed back in to see Cody, we placed that birthday picture at the head of his bed. We would point at the picture and began telling everyone, *"Cody will recover 100 percent and walk out of this hospital looking just like that."* We couldn't get any Christian programs on the television and we weren't about to look or watch or listen to anything else.

> ## We had to guard our minds and hearts.

The staff instructed us on the PICU procedures. The doors were secured and you gained access by pushing a button just outside the doorway. The attendant would come on the speaker and ask for your name and the name of the patient that you wanted to see. You had to wash your hands, in an area just on the other side of the entry doors, before going to the patient's bed. There could be no more than two at the bedside at any one time. Visiting hours ran all day, from 8:30 in the morning until 8:30 at night. The only times visitors were not allowed in were during staff shift changes. I was amazed at the long periods of time we could spend with our son.

Thursday, July 3, 1997—The Second Day

A tape player showed up on Cody's pillow. Even though he could not respond, his little spirit was hearing only what God said about him, we made sure of that.

> ## God responds to His Word and His Word *never* fails.

I knew my emotions wanted to take over, but now was not the time. Ted had learned from Kenneth Copeland, in the late 1970's, that "faith-filled words dominate the laws of death." Ted loved to listen to good Bible teaching. He would listen to Brother Copeland on the AM radio, (that's about all that was available back then) while fishing in West Galveston Bay. He would record the 15-minute broadcasts on a cassette and replay the message over and over until the message would become anchored in his spirit. He still has the tape from 1980 in which he learned *"faith-filled words dominate the laws of death."* We are forever grateful to Brother Copeland for that teaching.

> *"Faith-filled words dominate the laws of death!"*

Ted also remembered a teaching he heard from Jerry Savelle, in August 1978, in a tent meeting in Galveston, Texas. Brother Savelle was teaching from Psalm 112, about how an uncompromisingly righteous man *"is not moved by evil tidings"* (Psalm 112:6-7). Jerry said, "To put that in our modern day, Texas vernacular:

> **"Bad news don't shake him!"**

On the newly acquired cassette tape player, we would continually alternate scripture and Word tapes. We strategically placed the tape deck on Cody's pillow. When we weren't by his bedside, we instructed the nurses to keep the tapes playing. Friends began to bring us teaching tapes and music tapes also.

Days would go by that only a scripture would get me through. *I knew if I could find it in the Word, God would do it!* Ted and I had visitation rights any time of the day or night, except during two shift changes. It was such a blessing to be able to go in to see Cody almost anytime. That proved to be a great arrangement for us and also accommodated the many friends that came to see Cody, most of which were from out of town.

About 9:30 that morning, our pastor and staff care minister came to see us. As they arrived, Cody was being transported downstairs for a CAT scan and EEG. A transport team, complete with a doctor and several nurses, had to be with Cody during this procedure. Our pastor asked for the team to stop a minute, so he could lay hands and pray over Cody as he lay on the gurney. He commented that, "Cody had life in him and this was not a death sentence. Cody was going to live!"

Ted and I thought these medical tests were performed to see how *well* Cody was progressing. We didn't realize that the hospital was trying to document Cody as "brain dead'. When that was determined, the recommendation would be given to turn off the life support systems and get our permission to harvest his organs! I'm so glad we didn't really understand the procedure at the time.

Later that afternoon, a sharply dressed police officer walked into the family waiting room. He took one look at me and said, "Yea, you're the one. You either got religion real quick or you already had it." I didn't recognize Officer Bob when he came in the doorway, but he recognized me. He introduced himself to us as Bob Opperman, a Houston police officer. He and his fellow-officer, John McGowen, were taking some time off before going into work the day of the accident. They were the two jet skiers loading their crafts on the trailer when we first arrived at the lake. Carolyn had gone over to them to ask for their help. Bob caught a ride with a Jet Skier to the sailboat and John was the man clearing out the parking lot for the helicopter to land. Bob was the man that helped give Cody CPR. He came to the hospital as a follow up because he wasn't sure if Cody had made it. Upon arriving at the hospital and inquiring how to find us, the hospital security officer showed him the way. We were glad Bob had come to meet us and we were able to thank him personally for helping. We talked a while and filled in some of the missing pieces of the story. Officer Bob relayed his version of the rescue and how his life was impacted by this experience. Bob said he and Officer John (his partner) had been given some time off and were able to go into work a little late the previous day, so they decided to run the waves. It was part of God's rescue plan for us that day. He related how he had seen the television program "Rescue 911', but this was a first real-life experience for him. For the first time in his life, he saw a dead body come back to life. He said he actually saw life come back into Cody's body as I stood over him and spoke "Life come into Cody, I speak life into Cody." Bob said that throughout the evening after the accident, he had a lingering taste in his mouth of french fries or chicken. He couldn't get that taste out of his mouth. I told him how Cody had eaten chicken nuggets and fries on the way to the sailboat outing. He said he tried to drown the taste with several beers, but it just wouldn't go away. Bob's superior officer allowed him to take time off from work, to come from the far-west side of Houston, to visit Cody. That visit was only the first of many.

When our friends Roy, Lynette and Travis Waldrep, came up for a visit, they brought a camera. I guess the word had gotten out of my request for a camera, in order to document Cody's recovery in pictures. God was going to do a miracle and I wanted proof. I had our camera on the sailboat, but it had been water logged and ruined.

As Carolyn and Ed were leaving their home in Baytown, to come back to the hospital, the phone rang. It was Patsy Chapman, a friend from their church, calling to see if she could do anything for the family. During their Wednesday night church service, they had announced Cody had died. When Carolyn told her they were on their way back to the hospital, she was relieved to know Cody was still alive and quickly finished their conversation. Patsy had been in prayer that morning and asked the Lord to comfort the family. Then she saw a vision. Jesus was walking with a little boy through a beautiful meadow filled with flowers. As the two walked along side each other, Jesus was looking down and conversing with the little boy. Later, when Carolyn showed Patsy a picture of Cody, she immediately recognized the boy walking with Jesus as Cody. She exclaimed, "That's the little boy, that's the boy I saw walking with Jesus, as I was praying for the Brunt family!" The boy was wearing shorts, tee shirt, and tennis shoes; his hair was just exactly the same. Needless to say that was a great comfort to us, learning how God had everything in His control. We knew in our hearts that Cody went to heaven, but this vision confirms it. Ed was so faithful to come to the hospital everyday and sit with us. He answered the phone and brought me fruit and snacks. Whatever we needed, he was there to help. We took advantage of Ed's helpfulness to go to the hospital chapel during the shift changes. We would go to the chapel and walk, pray, and quote scriptures. I'd play the piano and sing. We would personalize songs for Cody. Some favorites were, "Look what the Lord has done, He healed Cody's body, He touched Cody's mind, He saved Cody just in time"; "There is nothing that Cody needs that He won't supply, there is nothing Cody needs that He won't provide cause we believe, yes we believe...and so I say to pneumonia move, and so I say to pneumonia get out of Cody..."I went to the enemy's camp and I took back what he (the devil) stole from me"; just to name a few. I noticed the surveillance cameras in the chapel and chuckled to myself to think someone was watching us and probably wondering what we were doing. How can these people be so positive in such a hard situation? We knew we had to stay built up and the times in the chapel were so strengthening. Ted and I would "have church', just the two of us. It never failed that as we entered the chapel, somebody would be leaving, and we would have the building all to ourselves. God was gracious even in the smallest detail.

> **It was important to keep things positive and not allow the heaviness of the situation to bring in doubt.**

As visitors came in, when we were in the sitting room, it was important to keep things positive and not allow the heaviness of the situation to bring in doubt. Every night before visiting time was over, those that were there would gather in a circle and pray, sing, and praise a while before leaving.

> **We knew we had to stay strong in the Lord and the power of His might!**

From the first night, we had asked friends to call the major ministries' prayer lines, as well as the local Christian radio station, to request prayer for Cody's recovery. I began to receive calls and faxes from out of town, out of state, even out of the country. Friends in Oklahoma, Botswana, Africa, and Bolivia contacted us. The 'gospel hot line' was definitely engaged! **PRAYER CHANGES THINGS AND CIRCUMSTANCES!** It was my joy to answer the phone with, "Miracle in motion, Cody's mom speaking." Later I received a T-shirt with that phrase on it from Sandi and Charlie Potter. I was so blessed to wear the message. That particular afternoon, we received a call from Dodie Osteen, wife of the late Pastor John Osteen, of Lakewood Church where I attended church in the late 70's and early 80's. A dear pastor-friend, Robert Dowdy, had called them about Cody. Dodie said they were praying for us and asked if we needed anything. I quickly replied, "Sleep!" The Lord answered that request that night. I began to sleep with the aid of a tape player. Things go much better if your brain has a little rest and your body has a little sleep. There was peace in my sleep now.

Brittany had to have a training session with the hospital staff to be allowed to go in and see Cody. The hospital social worker arranged the meeting with a staff member. She discussed the various medical apparatus that would be attached to Cody's body and their functions. Brittany listened and cooperated well. She was very calm, but eager to see her brother. When we brought her in to see Cody, she went right up to the bed, looked at him, and talked to him as though he could hear her. The doctor was right there, watching to make sure she could handle the situation. We were so proud of her bravery and the ease in which she supported her little brother. Even though he couldn't respond, she explained the drawings and crafts she had made for him. She would bring Cody pictures she had drawn and colored for each visit.

Friday, July 4th—Day Three

On day three, aspiration pneumonia set in strongly, with thick yellow secretions. Here was one more hurdle to cross. Cody's fever was spiking during the night. A chest x-ray was taken every morning. We waited for the results to come back. Again and again the results were "very congested". The pneumonia was getting worse. My nurse friend, Misty, had our authorization to call the nurse's station every morning and get an updated report. She called me to explain in everyday language what Cody was facing and give us specific prayer needs for that set of circumstances. After talking with me, Misty would call the church before the staff's prayer time and give them a report. Friends and neighbors knew to call the church, as a base, for a current status report of Cody's condition. As we had specific direction or symptoms to pray over, we would get the word out for prayer. I called them **'prayer targets'** and prayer without exception, shot them down. We saw victory each time!

I was by Cody's bed when the neurologist came in at 10:55 a.m. He told the nurse to stop the paralyzing medication, in order to get an accurate response from Cody. The ventilator setting was so high that too much movement from Cody could blow out his lungs. After a while, Cody began flinching. He vigorously moved his arms, legs, and tried to cough. He gagged a little. The doctor's report was "No withdrawal to painful stimuli". This was not a good report, but we believed it would change.

His blood pressure medication was decreased and sodium level treated. The paralyzing medication was administered again to help keep him calm. After watching this ordeal, I began praying that Cody would not remember the drowning and would have no fear of water. The nurses assured us that the medications of Versed and Vecuronium would keep him from remembering the PICU experience.

This was a very busy day with numerous visitors. It was the Fourth of July. The holiday allowed many friends, off from work, to come and visit. Our church had their annual picnic and activities. Numerous church friends and staff came to the hospital, either before or after the picnic. There is no way I can remember the entire host of people that visited that day. Whoever came by received instruction on the visitor entrance process, "Push the button, walk through the doors, wash your hands on the right, and turn left at the nurse's station. Cody's bed is #2 at the end." We wanted everyone who came to see

Cody to be able to go in and pray over him. I wish now I would have kept a visitor's log. Words cannot express how much true friendship counts during trying times.

Ted was not getting the rest he needed, so he made plans to go back to Texas City at night. We vacated the parent sleeping room that was assigned to us and moved into the family waiting room across from the PICU doors. This room had a window, bathroom, several chairs and a cot.

The Koneman family, former neighbors of ours, had their annual Fourth of July swimming party that evening. Brittany wanted to go and swim. I looked at Ted, he was confidant that she needed to go and get back in the water again. The Barry Barnes family was visiting at the time and offered to take her to the party. She enjoyed playing with their daughters and wanted to spend the night also. They promised to watch her carefully and we trusted Brittany to their care. She needed to get out and have fun, as any eight-year old should.

At the end of the day, I spent time alone with Cody. After kissing him good night, I retreated across the hall to the family waiting room. My faith was being stretched to the limit. Reality was setting in. As I opened the door to the empty room my emotions erupted like a volcano. I felt like I was trying to hold the whole world upon my shoulders. I walked over to the window. The sky was clear with a few stars shining and below was the view of the roof. I lifted my hands and head toward the ceiling and cried out to the Lord. I really needed some assurance that God was listening. I had remained strong through the many visitors that long day, but the medical reports were not getting any better. I reminded myself of scripture and assured myself that things would change. In the pit of my stomach was a cry of desperation. Jonah worshiped the Lord in the belly of the fish and was delivered, so I started to praise the Lord, thanking Him for healing Cody, and giving Him thanks for being such a powerful God. I walked over to the bed and looked at the phone. I was reminded of Mary Anne Copelin, who is a dear friend that lived in Houston. She was a powerful woman of God and a mighty prayer warrior. I was impressed to ask her to pray with me. I looked up her phone number and made the call. When she answered the phone, I remember blurting out how bad the pneumonia in Cody's body had accelerated and asked her to agree with me that his healing would manifest. The words were barely out of my mouth when she said very emphatically, **"It shall be."** There was no hesitation and no debate. She just said, **"It shall be."** That was good enough for me. The assurance that I so desperately needed engulfed me, and peace, once again, was restored to my soul.

Before retiring for the night, I walked back into PICU and told the night staff that if they needed me I'd be right across the hall. I wasn't going to leave the hospital until Cody woke up and said, "I'm hungry," like he was known to do. It seemed like Cody was always hungry at home. I'm sure the staff was well aware of our location across the hall, but I wanted to make sure.

I guess it is natural to question why an accident takes place. Hindsight is always 20/20. Cody's recovery was taking more time than I planned. This was my first night to be alone at the hospital. A little anxiety tried to overtake my emotions. I showed my weakness that night, as I questioned God with "Why Cody?" and "Was it my fault?" Had I done something to cause this calamity to come on Cody? Had I sinned in some way and brought this on my son? In the tenderness that only our Heavenly Father can show, He reminded me of the boy that was born blind (John 9). The disciples, his neighbors, the

Pharisees, and the Jews all questioned who had sinned and caused the blindness. Jesus forever settled the question. It wasn't the boy's, nor the parents, fault. Jesus said it happened that *"the works of God should be made manifest in him."* It felt like a two-ton weight lifted from my shoulders. No longer did I feel the guilt and responsibility of the accident. I knew that God would manifest His glory in our situation.

During that time, I began sleeping with the aid of a cassette player on my pillow. The only way I could sleep was by playing teaching tapes all night long; otherwise the accident kept racing through my mind. I would use the cassettes to silence the fears and feed my faith at the same time.

Saturday, July 5, 1997—Day Four

I was in the family room when one of the nurses brought me a specimen jar with one of Cody's teeth in it. Every morning they cleaned Cody and freshened up the linens. During the time they vacuumed his mouth, one of the loose teeth suctioned out. This was Cody's first tooth to lose. None of his teeth were even loose before the accident. I mentioned my concern to the nurse about getting the other loose teeth taken care of, so that Cody wouldn't swallow one. She looked at me very kindly and told me not to worry. She reminded me that Cody wasn't swallowing and it was posing no kind of danger. The dentists from the Texas Children's hospital were notified and would be coming later to check his teeth.

Later in the afternoon, several of our friends, the Wellers and Histo family, brought a big basket of goodies. It included some Christian tee shirts for Cody, as well as gifts, toiletries, snacks, etc. It was especially appreciated because right before they got there we were trying to find some lip balm for Cody's dry lips. It just happened that the basket had the Chap Stick we needed! God really thinks of everything!

The doctors were concerned about the drop in Cody's red blood count. They suggested giving Cody a blood transfusion. We wanted to be certain of a healthy blood supply, so preparations began for donating that afternoon. It takes two days for the proper procedures to be done on donated blood, before it can be used, and we wanted the blood available as soon as possible. We learned all the necessary procedures and information about donations. Since the hospital didn't have the facility there, we made arrangements to visit the blood bank with all the A-positive friends we could find.

In all this blood discussion, the conversation turned to a question of whether or not Cody had been anointed with oil. James 5:14 instructs that the elders of the church should anoint with oil and pray the prayer of faith over them. I couldn't remember if that had been done, so our friend Karen Villarreal went down to the gift shop and bought some oil; baby oil, which was all they had, but that would do.

The visitors present at the time, Karen and her sister, Lisa Santos, and Patti Moore, a dear friend who lived in Houston, were checked for their blood type. I didn't know my way around Houston well. Patti knew right where the blood bank was so she drove me over. Roland Kelley drove Debbie Benson and Lisa Santos over in his truck. The four of us (Roland, Debbie, Lisa and I) gave blood as "designated donors" so Cody would be sure and get our blood. We all were in our chairs happily giving the 'gift of life'. As we were talking, Debbie and Lisa commented on how much this proved their love for Cody. I knew they were just kidding. Their act of love was priceless. The next day at church, word got out Cody needed blood donors and several others gave at other blood banks.

> **I would use the cassette tapes to Silence the fears and feed my faith at the same time.**

After donating the blood, the others went back to the hospital, and Patti took me to eat. The nurse at the blood bank told me to eat a good meal with meat, since I was boarderline anemic. I knew that I needed to eat, but I wasn't hungry in the least. Patti drove me to a Steak and Ale restaurant and I ordered my favorite steak, a filet mignon. During the meal, Patti tried to keep me preoccupied with conversation, but my heart was back with Cody.

> **In the natural his recovery seemed such an impossible situation, but I would not allow my mind to dwell on the severity of our circumstances.**

At one point during the meal, I remember looking up at a couple sitting across the room. After they were served their meal, they bowed their heads and blessed their food. On our way out of the restaurant, I walked over to their table. I was looking for help anywhere I could get it. While choking back tears, I explained about Cody and asked them to pray for him. Without hesitation, they immediately took my hand and said a prayer agreeing with me for his recovery. I was not shy when it came to my son's life.

> **My face was set on his total healing and I would do everything possible to see it come to pass.**

Back at the hospital that evening, my obstetrician and his wife, Dr. Richard and Marvia Walker, visited. Ted was by Cody's bed when they came in PICU. When Ted saw them he fought back tears of joy. He said he could "feel' the atmosphere change as these people of "faith' came into the room. Dr. Walker wanted to know specific things to pray over Cody. We were able to talk with one of Cody's neurologists to get specific medical conditions and reports. Ted and I were so encouraged with their visit and show of concern and love. The night Cody was born, Dr. Walker had walked Ted through Cody's delivery. Ted always joked that, "I pulled Cody out and Dr. Walker still charged us $2,000!" More visitors arrived while Dr. Walker was there, so he phoned later to discuss medical details he had obtained from the neurologist and prayed over it some more. He told me how important it was to pray specifically and gave me names and descriptions of certain neurological functions to speak out in prayer. I got a paper and pen and wrote them down. We were to pray for:

I.   **Normal cognitive abilities—cognition**
II. **Normal fine motor skills**
III. **Normal Cerebellum**
IV. **Normal Cerebrum**
V.   **Normal, active subconscious**
VI. **Normal short-term and long-term memory**
VII. **No remembrance of the accident**

He prayed with me over the phone and hung up. My mind was racing with unfamiliar medical terms, but God knew them all and the prayer of agreement put the restoration process in motion.

Another nurse friend, Barbara Ward, had an idea to have pastor preach with a pair of socks in his pocket. In the Bible, Acts 19:11,12, Paul prayed over handkerchiefs and they were taken and placed on ill patients. The anointing was transferred through cloths. She brought a pair of socks that evening and we wrote "Satan's under my feet" on one and "My victory is complete" on the other. She took them to our pastor the next morning and he agreed to preach with them in his pocket. The anointing can be transferred through material and this was a unique way to do it. It was a great idea.

Ted was alone and standing by Cody's bed when he asked God, "What about the bad reports and words that the doctors and nurses would speak over him contrary to our confession?" The Lord referred him to Romans 3:3-4, ***"For what if some did not believe? Shall their unbelief make the faith of God without effect? God forbid: yea, let God be true, but let every man a liar; as it is written, That thou mightest be justified by THY SAYINGS, and mightest overcome when thou art judged."*** At this point Ted and I were in authority over our son's welfare and we were standing by the Word of God. As we guarded our mouths and spoke God's Words over Cody, it would nullify the evil reports.

Roland called to check on our little man. That day, his wife, Linda, and friend, Yolanda Johnson, went over to our apartment and did the laundry and general house cleaning. What precious friends God had given us! This had been another long, busy day. I went back in to see Cody before retiring for the evening and getting some much needed rest. Being alone at night didn't bother me too much. By the time everyone was gone at night, I was ready to lay down a while and enjoy the quiet. This room, across the hall from the PICU doors, was such a blessing to have as a rest haven. We placed pictures of Cody and a current 'prayer target' list on the glass window on the door. We also placed pictures of Cody in his baseball uniform and notes people would stop by and add.

Sunday, July 6, 1997—Day Five

First thing in the morning, I went in to check on my boy. I greeted the night shift that was about to go home. X-rays taken that morning showed increasing infiltration. The pneumonia was still present.

During the morning service, our pastor preached with Cody's socks in his suit pocket. After church, "Aunt Barb' brought the socks and put them on Cody's feet. With each of our children, 'Aunt' Barbara had come to the hospital and put their first socks on. Once again she was the "sock lady'. The staff and visitors had some questions of what the phrases meant, so we explained…What a witness! At this point, we were doing anything the Bible said we could.

As I was watching one of the nurses' work on Cody, for the first time I questioned why Cody's bed was kind of out in the open. I wondered why he wasn't placed in one of the nice, quiet, glassed-in rooms on the perimeter of the unit. She said when Cody arrived, they weren't expecting him to live through the night. She continued to explain that if they needed to pull in more equipment, it would allow more room for the trauma team to work on him. I'm glad I didn't know that a few days earlier. By this time we were getting very familiar with the caregivers and they with us. They knew our beliefs, but most didn't understand them or our methods. They were doing what they were trained to do and we were doing what the Word instructed us to do. Ted spent much of his visiting time by Cody's bedside; quoting scriptures that promised healing, deliverance, safety, etc. My husband is very well versed in scripture. I like to refer to him as my "walking concordance'. I guess you could say he has a "photographic memory'. Ted likes to say that everyone has a photographic memory, but some people just have the lens cap glued on! Seriously, he has spent many hours listening to the Word and reading the Word.

Ted often stood at the bed and confessed aloud what God's Word had to say about Cody's condition. He would turn to the wall and visualize Cody's angel. The Bible says that children's angels always behold the face of the Father (Matthew 18:10). After he concluded, Ted would dispatch the angel to report to the Father and tell Him what Cody's dad was saying about him. Also in the Word, the angels hearken to the voice of God's Word. That was the Word in Ted's mouth. I'm sure the nurses thought he was a little "off", but spiritually we were "right on".

> Take heed that you despise not one of these little ones; for I say unto you, That in heaven their angels do always behold the face of my Father which is in heaven. Matthew 18:10

That afternoon brought another constant flow of visitors. Many had gone to church that morning for service, ate lunch, and came to the hospital. I stayed in the waiting room and visited, while two at a time went into Cody's bedside. We encouraged them to talk to Cody just as if he could respond. In a coma, the patient can hear but cannot respond. When you do all you can do, you have to trust God to do what you can't do.

We did our best to stage the atmosphere for a miracle. God inhabits (sits enthroned in) the praises of his people (Psalm 22:3). We didn't praise God for *what* happened to Cody, but we praised God *'in'* the circumstances, because we knew His promises were true.

> *"In everything give thanks:*
> *for this is the will of God in Christ Jesus concerning*
> *you."*
> *I Thessalonians 5:18*

Monday, July 7th—Day Six

As always, I went in about 5:00 a.m. to see how he did during the night. The nurses, as always, answered my questions and respected our concerns. At 6:30 a.m., during the shift change, I freshened up for the day ahead. I used that time to pray and read the Word to maintain my spiritual strength.

When I came back in at 8:00 a.m., Cody had an additional IV. It was red blood. He was getting my blood! The nurse was cleaning Cody and asked me if I'd like to help. His feet were beginning to withdraw and turn in. I asked the nurse about it, even though I knew this indicated brain damage. I refused to receive it! It was subject to change! As I rubbed his legs and arms with lotion, I prayed and spoke to them to "be strong and healthy limbs" and "Cody was going to be an athlete to show God's glory some day". His ankles were developing pressure sores where they laid on the sheets. I was shown how to swab out his mouth and use a fluoride-coated sponge to clean his teeth. (At home, Cody was diligent to always brush and floss his teeth before bed every night without being told.) We began propping his legs up with pillows and alternating their positions.

Lori Weller's mother, Mrs. Ivey, sent a stuffed lion and we used him to prop up lines, limbs, hoses, etc. It really was a very useful lion. Helium balloon bouquets surrounded his bed, since flowers are prohibited in ICU. Little notes, sent from well wishers, were taped on the walls. These were constant reminders of their love and prayers.

Cody was given his second EEG that day. I was there and watched the procedure. The technician used a little fine sandpaper on the skin areas where the electrodes were placed, all 27 of them! I watched intently while the machines recorded the brain waves. I was so optimistic. As I talked with the technician, I commented, "At least there weren't any flat lines!" He didn't comment. There were all kinds of up and down lines showing some kind of activity. The technician just smiled and said he couldn't comment; "It would be against hospital policy." They tried to wean Cody off some of the sedatives, for more accurate readings on the test. His blood pressure would spike up and medications were increased. I reasoned that Cody was somehow trapped in his body and was trying to express himself, but the sedations were keeping him frustrated and that's why the blood pressure would increase. During the test, the neurologist came and asked Cody to open his eyes and it looked like he tried. I stood near and tried to persuade him to open his eyes as well. "Come on Cody, open your eyes, Mommy's here." The doctor continued with his examination. Cody's eyes were retracting equally to light and now grimaced to painful stimuli. He wrote on the chart, "neurological improvement". Dr. Frates was standing there at this time, also, and his comment was **"I believe he has a good chance of a significant recovery."** That was music to my ears! Up to this point, not many good comments were given to us. The sedatives had to be re-administered before the test was over. Cody was getting very agitated.

Later on, another team of doctors came to the bed. They were concerned about infection, other than the pneumonia. The antibiotics weren't attacking this infection. Several doctors came to the bed and discussed possible causes. Now I understand why physicians use the term "practicing medicine". They were playing out several "what if" scenarios. As I listened, I knew God knew exactly what the source of the infection was and HE could either fix it or show them. That day, Cody started taking nourishment through a stomach feeding tube. The nurse had trouble getting it positioned correctly and x-rays were taken frequently to watch this situation. Several times a new stomach feeding tube was put in place.

Tuesday, July 8th—Day Seven

I was sitting by Cody's bed at 11:20 a.m. when two dentists, from the Children's Hospital next door, came over. I was asked to leave as they worked on Cody and extracted the second and third loose teeth. I never thought this was the way he would loose his first teeth. It was a good thing he didn't know what was going on at this point. Just last month he had to have stitches in his toe and you could hear him scream all over the emergency room. He doesn't like needles or anything medical. Now Cody was missing three of his upper front teeth.

The phone rang incessantly. People somehow got the number at Cody's bedside phone in PICU, in the family waiting room, and occasionally we were summoned down the hall to the pay phones, in the lobby by the elevators. Several times people we didn't even know called. I remember one man introduced himself as a jet skier that was out on the lake the day of the accident. He and his daughter witnessed the rescue and wanted to inquire about Cody's progress.

Our nurse friend, Teresa Hooter, had the afternoon off from work. She came up and sat by Cody's bed and read scriptures to him. She wanted to give me a break and asked what I would like her to do. It sure helped me too. Her family almost cancelled their vacation because of the accident, but we insisted they keep their plans and I promised to keep in touch with her mom. She brought some souvenirs from their trip for Cody.

Three officers from the Houston Fire Department of the base at NASA visited Cody. These were some of the paramedics that responded to the 911 call. I didn't think to write down their names. Their thoughtfulness and concern was much appreciated for our little boy. The Life Flight nurse, Lynn Ethridge and Life Flight paramedic, Kim Cone, visited several times. They were concerned during the flight that day that Cody wouldn't make it to the hospital. Lynn commented how his lungs were 'so congested'.

Even with the strict visiting rules and regulations, there was a steady stream of friends and family giving us strength and support. We felt like Moses in the Bible, with Aaron and Hur, along side holding up our hands to see the victory. Talk about a 'support group'; we had one!

Medically we were making progress. The blood transfusion increased the red blood count from 8.8 on Monday to 12.3 on Tuesday. The doctors were very pleased. Cody's legs and arms were cold, so I kept socks on his feet and gave his extremities massages. His fever went to 103 during the night. The central venous catheter was removed and sent to the lab to determine if it was the possible cause of infection. They took Cody off the Dopamine for his blood pressure. Things were slowly beginning to change.

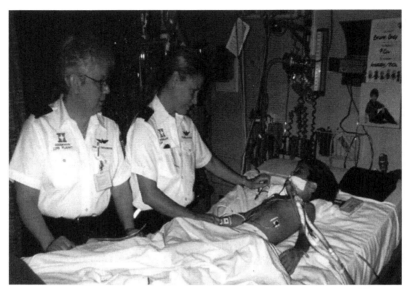

Life Flight nurses Judy & Lynn visiting Cody.

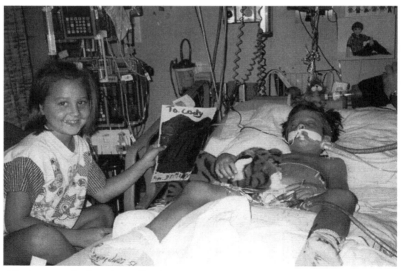

**Brittany bringing Cody pictures. *Note socks on his feet
"Satan is defeated"; "My victory is complete."**

Chapter 4

Fighting the Good Fight of Faith

Wednesday, July 9th—Day Eight

As I held my normal position by Cody's bed, the doctors had their morning conference. They commented that over the last twelve hours his condition had improved. The infection had been targeted, antibiotics were changed, ventilator settings were lowered, and the lung secretions were clearer! That was good news to hear! Cody was, by that time, getting 100 percent of his nourishment from the stomach feeding tube; one less IV bag.

Ted was spending more time with Brittany and he called me from home that morning. He said that God spoke to him in prayer and that Cody's condition would change **"suddenly"**. He referred to Mark 7:24-30. Jesus would move time for Cody! I agreed with that report. I was more than ready for things to improve.

Later on that evening, the stomach feeding tube had to be removed and Cody was put back on IV nutrition. The tube was moving and getting out of position. The nasal secretions were increasing, but they were white, clear, and foamy. I watched the inhalation therapists come, as they did daily, and pound on Cody to loosen the congestion in the lungs. Different therapists had their own style of pounding; some used their hands while others used special paddles. They even turned Cody on his stomach and tilted the head of the bed down to promote dissipation of the fluid.

Mike Nickols, Cody's T-Ball baseball coach, came to see him. He relayed how he had been out of town and had just received the news of the accident. Coach Mike is a fine Christian man, as well as the best T-Ball coach ever. Mike and Ted went in by Cody's bed and visited for a long time. There was a profound difference between Cody's energetic baseball playing and his present condition in that hospital bed. At that point, baseball was a distant memory. Mike had been Cody's coach for two seasons. Cody was awarded the "Rookie of the Year" trophy, during the previous month at the T-Ball awards night. Cody was a "natural' when it came to baseball. Mike enjoyed Cody's enthusiasm, attentiveness, and ability to listen and follow directions. Ted and Coach Mike prayed together, believing that Cody would fully recover and play again the next season.

Later on that evening, I went in to kiss Cody goodnight. Dr. Rebecca Watson was at the foot of his bed, writing on his chart. She "unofficially' commented to me that if I needed something to pray for that night to pray for Cody's temperature to remain normal throughout the night. She said, "That's what I am going to pray for". Her concern and sincerity impressed me. Dr. Watson had been on Cody's case from the first night. All we could do at this point was to pray and ask for wisdom for the doctors in treating our little "Codybug."

The accident was a week in history by this time. So much had transpired. So many hurdles were behind us and our faith was still strong for Cody's 100 percent recovery. The various notes on the door of the family waiting room was a reminder of so many people supporting and encouraging us during that time.

Thursday, July 10th—Day Nine

Cody was scheduled for a MRI that day. Brittany had qualified for the regional TAAF track meet, and Ted insisted that I leave the hospital for a while to watch her. I hadn't even gone downstairs to the cafeteria, much less out of the hospital. The only time I left was to go give blood. I was determined to be by his side when he woke up. We arranged for Ed to come and relieve me. Ed had been so faithful to come and help out in any way he could. He was willing to do whatever needed to be done. Carolyn tried coming to the hospital with Ed everyday, at first, but the emotional pressures were taking a toll. She felt she would be more helpful by staying home and praying. Wallace had gone back to work to keeping his time occupied and cope with the emotional stress of the accident. I went in to Cody's bed as usual that morning. It was quiet and I sat holding his hand, praying over him. I wouldn't be coming in after the shift change, so I had to use this time to set the stage for this important day. As the new shift came on duty, I delayed leaving until the last minute. I went across the hall and waited for Ed. The phone rang at 7:45. Ed was on his mobile phone and was pulling up in the parking lot. I told him I'd be right down.

As I closed the door, a little yellow post-it note caught my eye. The note read, *"Lil Dr. Cody Brunt, I want you to know that you are not in this warfare alone. The Youth Department of Kashmere Gardens Baptist Church is on its knees in prayer for you as well as myself. Stay strong and hold on because your deliverance is on its way!"* Signed Ronald Curtis, patient escort.

Well that did it! I fell apart and started to cry. I had bottled my emotions pretty well throughout the week following the accident, but to realize people we didn't even know were pulling for Cody touched my heart. By the time I got down to Ed's car, he took one look at me and asked what was the matter. I reached for him, fell on his shoulder, and cried. The whole situation was getting to me. We hugged and he assured me everything was going to be all right. I told him I'd be back as soon as the track meet was over and if anything came up to call on my mobile phone.

As I pulled out of the parking lot, the car radio was on our favorite Christian station, KSBJ. At that moment, I realized that this was the first time I had listened to the radio in a week. There was a whole other world out there. The sun was shining and the weather was hot and humid. Houston is notorious for all three! One thing about a hospital is that it is a world of its own. The outside world could be falling apart, but you'd never know it in the confines of a hospital. Hospital life goes on 24 hours a day and doesn't skip a beat.

I was running a little early on time. As I drove into Texas City, I decided to stop by to check on the construction progress of our new home. I drove up the quiet street to a beautiful wooded lot, where we planned raise *both* children. I opened the gate and proceeded to walk through the framed structure. The roof was on and the house was at the "dried in" stage. I looked at the bare wood frames over the doors and windows and focused on the scriptures I had written a few short weeks before. "No weapon formed against you will prosper"…"He will bless your sleep for you are taught of the Lord"…"With long life you will be satisfied"…"God has not given us the spirit of fear, but of power, love and a sound mind."

I walked down the hall to Cody's room. I spoke to the walls and said "Cody is going to come back healed and whole and will live happily in this room. He will have fun times playing in this room." My emotions wanted to scream out. I needed a release, but I couldn't allow myself to get down and doubt or look at the circumstances. The circumstances *had* to change and my son had to be normal again, but when?

> **My emotions wanted to scream out.**
> **I needed a release, but I couldn't allow myself to get**
> **down and doubt or look at the circumstances.**

I left and drove on to the Texas City High School football stadium. This was a regional track meet. People from the surrounding regions were there. I arrived, parked the car, and began to look for Ted and Brittany, but my heart was not there. I wanted to be with Cody, but Brittany needed me too. As I walked in the open air, I saw familiar parks and recreation personnel. I tried my best to smile and stay on top of things. If I tried to talk, all I could do was cry. I watched as the strong, healthy, athletic kids energetically warmed up and got ready to compete. Many of Cody's team members didn't even know he was in the hospital in a coma. I was able to tell some of the parents the story, but for the most part, all I could do was smile and walk on by them.

I found Brittany and Ted sitting in the stands under a big new umbrella. It was very hot! I was trying to be up for our daughter and encourage her. It was a long morning of races. She placed in the preliminary heats. The finals would be run after lunch. The three of us went out for lunch, then Brittany and I went to the apartment to freshen up before the finals. The lunch break stretched into the afternoon. Ted went back to the hospital and I stayed to watch Brittany compete. She placed second in the 50-meter race and was presented a silver medal on the victor's stand. I was careful to capture the moment on the video and still cameras. When she came over to me, she said, "Mom, I won this for Cody." We went to the apartment, cleaned up, and drove back to the hospital.

By this time, I was ready to hear some good news and see some progress. Brittany went over to Cody's bed and showed him the silver medal dangling from her hand. She told him that she ran for him and won the medal for him. The nurses looked on with amazement.

I had two phone calls that evening from special, long-time friends, Rachel Burchfield and Bertie Jones, who really encouraged and prayed with me. The Lord knows just what you need, when you need it!

After Ted and Brittany went back home, several friends came up to visit that evening. One was my "TV watch dog', Regina Nilsson. This friend saw the breaking newscast the day of the accident. The CBS affiliate in Houston implied that the accident might have been alcohol related. She refused to let that implication go unchallenged, so she immediately called the station. She informed them that *she knew* the family and it was in no way an alcohol-related accident. They heeded her protest, retracting that statement on the next telecast that evening. As she told me of this incident, I was so thankful for friends who defend and support us. We never saw the newscasts until we got home and watched the footage friends recorded for us. The news coverage aired on all three major Houston stations. The news helicopters hovering over the scene that day were quick to capture the incident.

The family waiting room was filled with "goodies' and munchies friends had brought. I had a supply of my favorite Dr. Peppers that had to be brought in from the outside. The beverage became a precious commodity. We feasted on the love and prayers that surrounded us. It was almost like being in a cocoon of love and care.

Also that evening, several friends from church came in after visiting hours. Don Stidham, a friend that has become a second father to me, posed as Cody's grandfather, and Scarlet Brents, Pat Martin, and Brenda Osborn were all "family" as well. Don persuaded the nurses to let them in to see Cody and pray over him even after hours!

Cody's blood pressure began to spike up again, so his sedation was increased but now the arterial catheter was removed. The feeding tube had to be repositioned. The report of the MRI taken that morning came back that evening. It confirmed Cody had a **"sinus infection!"** Wow, **that** *was* **GOOD** *news!* Finally, things seemed to be looking up. The tests were beginning to reflect what we had been confessing.

Friday, July 11th, Day Ten

Little did I realize that morning what a monumental day it would become. The nurses reported to me that Cody had a good night. During the night, he became agitated and the hypertension required Ativan and Clonidine. That morning, I helped bathe Cody, put lotion on, and message his arms and legs. I sang and read to him as usual. Cody was beginning to move and get in different positions in the bed. This was a good sign, after seeing him so still and motionless. They were trying to wean Cody off the paralyzing sedations. He was beginning to open his eyes some and trying to focus occasionally. On his chart, they stated that he had, as the doctors put, "purposeful arm movement'.

Ted came up mid-morning and told me that they were going to try taking Cody off the ventilator. For some reason, that didn't register with me. I must have been talking on the phone or something. About 3 o'clock that afternoon we were not allowed to be with our son for this procedure and the nurse asked us to leave Cody's bedside.

About 3:30 p.m. they extubated (removed the ventilator tube from his lungs) Cody. We have the report of the blow by blow account. He started breathing on his own! They weren't expecting Cody to talk for a day or so because of the possible damage to the vocal chords. With the breathing tube in his larynx so long, the least he would have to suffer was a very raw throat.

Cody showed signs of agitation with any noise or verbal stimulation. We were not allowed to see him for the remainder of the afternoon and evening. He didn't talk or respond immediately, but at least he began to breathing on his own. The reports show that he became "agitated and combative with tactile or verbal stimuli'. Cody was physically restrained to the bed during this time. I couldn't stand the separation from my son, so I went in and stood at the nurse's desk occasionally, looking from a distance. Being kept from comforting him and leaving him all alone was so difficult. What could be going through his mind waking up in a strange place, among strange people? The area around his bed was kept dark. The reports were that the thrashing behavior was the result of brain damage, but I knew that our little boy would be fine and I knew it was the sedative withdrawal that caused that behavior.

James Benson and another minister, Jimmy Kirby, came to see him late that night. The three of us watched from the nurse's station, away from his bed. Watching from a distance was painful and every mother molecule in me wanted to reassure Cody that it was all going to be all right. The scarcity of visitors that night was a good thing, since we were not permitted by Cody's bed. It stretched into a very long evening.

Saturday, July 12th—Day Eleven

My first action in the morning was to check in on Cody. It had seemed like days since we had seen our little boy. I was careful to stop at the nurse's station for instructions and a report on Cody's status. The nurse gave me a report of the night and escorted me to his bed. The nurse said he had been asking for his daddy and saying "no". I talked to him, but he didn't respond to me at the time. It was so good to see him breathing on his own. The tube was out of his mouth and the ventilator machine was taken away from the bedside. At least there was one less line going into his little body. Cody was still restrained, but I could stroke his forehead and talk softly in his ear, trying to give him reassurance. Dr. Rebecca Watson came by his bed and described more about the extubation procedure. She was the doctor in charge at the time of the procedure. Cody did well and started breathing on his own. She told me that following the procedure, as she was writing up the report, Cody made an audible comment to the nurse beside his bed. He said, "Yes Ma'am," and it was loud enough for Dr. Watson to hear it at the desk nearby. Cody was a well-mannered boy before the accident and his manners were still intact. She said she jumped up and ran over to see if what she thought that she heard was real. It was. Cody was talking! She was so excited that Cody was coming around. The doctor continued to explain that if he had not started to breathe on his own, a tracheal tube would have been installed to get the ventilator tube out of his mouth and assist his breathing. The ventilator must be removed after ten days because of the damage it does to the vocal chords. We have had friends and family on ventilators for only a day or two and they suffered raw throats and raspy voices for several days afterward.

Cody never complained of a sore throat at all. I stood there and relished that good report. The day was off to a great start!

Later, as I was reading and talking to Cody, the neurologist came in and proceeded to perform some tests. Cody responded to the pain stimuli this time. Now Cody looked around the room. He talked a little. He replied, "fine," when asked how he was. He told the doctor, "I need to go to the bathroom." Cody got agitated when we told him that he couldn't get out of the bed yet. We tried to explain his "automatic' bathroom (catheter) that was attached to him. He couldn't follow commands yet, but Cody was coming back!

One of the nurses asked if I wanted to hold him. What a question! My arms ached to hold my little Codybug again. They pulled up a rocker and I got all propped up and ready. As they handed him to me, it looked like Cody had grown two inches. His legs were so long! I rocked him as the nurse took a vial of blood and inserted another feeding tube. I couldn't look at that part. I just kept on singing to Cody little songs we had made up.

Dr. Watson walked back over and enjoyed seeing Cody's progress. She was very glad to see his improvement. From the first night of the accident, she had been on Cody's case, so she was well aware of the importance of this moment. When Ted came up later that morning and rounded the corner—there we were—rocking in the chair. I was singing and looking at Cody! At this time, Cody still did not open his eyes much or respond, but we were on the way. Things were looking UP!

We were glad to have him off of the respirator, but we weren't prepared for the withdrawals that followed. Cody was started on Methadone and Clonidine, to bring him gradually off the medications. Ativan was prescribed for Benzo withdrawal.

Ted let me know we had some visitors, to let him hold Cody a while so I could go visit in the waiting room. I was walking on air as I came out of PICU to visit with friends that had just arrived. It was a joy to be able give some good news updates and to send the visitors in one at a time. Some of Ted's co-workers, from the Amoco Texas City Refinery, brought a big basket of goodies and toys for Cody to enjoy. Friends and fellow church members, Dee and Larry Delgado, were in the family room waiting to see us as well. I wanted to visit more, but plans were being made to transfer Cody into a private room. I had to start packing our belongings from the family waiting room and move on to a private room down the hall. Cody was beginning to respond to us! Soon we were informed of Cody's new room. I thought that was a quick move, but they were in charge. Cody was still connected to IV's, oxygen, and feeding tubes. We started loading up the area around Cody's bed. By 3 o'clock that afternoon, we were out on the floor, in a private room. Carolyn and Ed arrived just in time to help carry a load of things to the room. Ted carried Cody in his arms. We had quite a procession going down the hall and around the corner from PICU.

It was Saturday and we had a busy evening of visitors. We tried to keep things quiet for Cody. One of the visitors brought up a blue tee shirt that had "Miracle in Motion" on the front and "Cody's Mom" on the back. That's the way I had been answering the phone when anyone called. Charlie and Sandie Potter had the shirt made for me. It was a sweet expression of love that not only warmed my heart, but also served as a witness to others around us. Wallace had come to visit and got to see his nephew awake for the first time. He was glad to see such progress, but witnessed Cody's thrashing fits. Carolyn and I were trying to hold Cody down on the bed. Wallace immediately recognized his behavior as drug withdrawals. I was consoled a little just to realize that what we had been thinking was truly the problem. We never received these 'fits' as brain damage from the accident, but a direct result of the many medications Cody had been on.

Carolyn offered to stay with me through the night. She knew I'd need help and Ted was not prepared to stay. With Cody awake now, we weren't going to let these symptoms dampen our enthusiasm.

It was a long, sleepless night for us. Cody was calling out and thrashing some. We'd sing to him softly, or pray, or whatever it took to calm him. I sat on a chair beside his bed and kept my arm on his arm all through the night. No one prepared us for this part. The location of the room allowed us to hear the take off and landing of the Life Flight helicopters. Sirens from ambulances outside could be heard also. When Cody would hear one, he'd tell me, "Pray Mommy." (We had a regular habit of praying when we saw an ambulance, with their flashing lights, as we drove down the highway. I would always pray a prayer of protection and help for the people involved. We had done that so often that he was responding to those sounds.) It was a tough night, but little did I know that it would get tougher! The first night was not so bad. Neither Carolyn nor I got any sleep. It was a small price to pay to have Cody back.

Sunday, July 13th—Day Twelve

The sun finally came up! We made it through the first night in the private room. It was Sunday morning so I turned on the TV to see if there were any church services to watch. I found one. I pointed to the preacher and asked Cody who was that preaching on the television. He quickly recognized the familiar face and said without hesitation, "Brother Osteen." I was ecstatic! His brain is functioning!

The nurse came in and checked Cody's blood oxygen reading and turned off the oxygen valve at 8:30 a.m. She came back an hour later. After checking his oxygen level, she took the breathing tube off his nose. One more line off! We unpacked some family home videos Ted had brought up to help Cody's memory recall. Cody enjoyed seeing himself. He laughed and had a good time. Carolyn and I enjoyed every moment.

God was putting a new brain in Cody's head!

The neurologist came in mid-morning. During the exam, Cody could accurately respond. He could say his own name, as well as recognize us and say our names. He intermittently followed commands, but not consistently. His speech was slightly slurred.

Visitors and family came in that afternoon and we tried to keep Cody as calm and quiet as possible. He would cry out occasionally. The devil tried to tell me he was having flashbacks of the drowning, but I wasn't going to allow that. Cody didn't like using a urinal. He wanted to go to the bathroom in the *bathroom*. Later that afternoon, I had stepped out of the room and went down the hall for a while. Upon returning to the room, I noticed Cody had started crying on Uncle Dewey's (Ted's older brother) shoulder. That was the first show of emotion Cody had displayed. We could only guess what had caused that outburst of emotion. Was it because he may have realized that his front teeth were missing and became self-conscious of it? At that point, Cody couldn't tell us why he was crying. I tried to console him and reassure him that we were there and wouldn't leave him.

When Ted arrived, Cody wanted to sit in Daddy's lap. After a while, Cody started squirming. He wasn't satisfied until he got his feet on the floor. We realized that he wanted to stand up. I couldn't help but notice how skinny his legs were next to daddy's muscular ones. During these last days, he had lost some weight, but his little bird legs looked beautiful to me as they were holding him up shakily. Praise God, he was standing! While he was sitting in Daddy's lap, Cody had a runny bowel movement and got Daddy's clothes soiled. His 'plumbing' was all working now! Ted left to go home, clean up, and prepare to stay the night with me. After the previous rough night Carolyn and I had, I knew I needed some reinforcements.

That evening, Cody was in constant motion, talking incoherently, needing constant supervision and reassurance. Our two nurse friends, Misty and Aunt Barb stayed a while and observed Cody's behavior. We tried everything to calm Cody down. We would prop him up with pillows in a red wagon the hospital had and pull him around the hallway, to have a change of scenery from the room. Ted and I were out in the hall, pulling Cody in the wagon when some friends from La Porte, Linda and Jim Searcy, walked up. We asked them to pray with us for Cody's calmness and rest throughout the night. We tried all kinds of distractions to comfort Cody when these attacks of hyperactivity hit. The doctors prescribed Ativan to help with these 'fits'. It was very hard for Ted and I to watch our little boy not be his gentle little self. We spoke to those lying symptoms and commanded them to leave. Things rocked along pretty well until about 4:00 a.m. Cody began 'bouncing' off the walls. Ted decided to put the restraints back on Cody's limbs, to protect him from hurting himself and to take a break. That picture of our gentle little boy, restrained to the bed and left alone, was so difficult to accept.

> **We spoke to those lying symptoms and commanded them to leave.**

It was heart breaking to see him thrash around and be so despondent. We were exhausted from all our unsuccessful efforts at calming Cody. I kept telling myself that this was not the Cody we knew nor the Cody we would eventually have back. Ted and I took a walk down the hall and tried to build each other up.

Monday, July 14th—Day Thirteen

We didn't get much rest at all during that night, but Cody seemed to settle down some by early morning. For breakfast, Cody enjoyed eating small chips of ice. This was the first thing he got to take in orally. The morning started with a flurry of activity. The physical therapist came to evaluate Cody's physical skills. She had him stand by the bed. Then she asked him if he could walk. I thought to myself, "My goodness, lady, he's been asleep for nine days, just let the boy wake up!"

The therapist was persistent, so we started from the room and walked to a playroom down the hall. Ted was rolling Cody's IV poll and I was flashing pictures with the camera. This was a moment I wanted to capture on film! Cody did very well. As we were walking down the hall, the Osterholms, (some former neighbors that are like the kid's grandparents) arrived and saw us walking down the hall. It was a great change since the first time they visited Cody in PICU. Wow, were they surprised to see us strolling down the hall! They followed us down to the playroom. They had play tables in the room with various toys. Cody wasn't following directions very well. He couldn't put the simplest puzzles together. The therapists made their reports noting how Cody sat up in the chair, how he supported himself, (a little crooked at the time) walked, and all his physical motions. That was all right. Cody had made such progress in two days that we rejoiced in his current level of recovery. We barely made it back to the room when the speech therapist arrived. She gave Cody applesauce and watched him eat and swallow. Everything went well and other foods were added to his diet. Cody's eyes were dilated somewhat and he stared at us a lot, but we believed the messages were registering in his brain.

Nurse Sally, one of Cody's inhalation therapists in PICU, stopped by to see his progress. It was so good to report his improvement and see her genuine concern for her patient. She had worked so hard with Cody while he had pneumonia in PICU.

Some rehabilitation people from the Texas Institute for Research and Rehabilitation (TIRR) came and expressed their desire to transfer Cody to their hospital, to further assist him in his recovery time. The head doctor had told us that the Hermann staff had done about all they could do for him there. They wanted our permission to transfer Cody to TIRR. Things started moving in that direction. The staff called our insurance company and made the arrangements.

About 2:00 p.m., Cody wanted to take a bath with Daddy. It was the easiest way to make sure Cody was stable in the water. As a baby, this had been a regular evening activity for Cody and Ted. I would not allow myself to think that Cody had digressed to a baby again. We looked at him and saw him restored to perfect health. Cody was placed on a purred diet. About 3 o'clock that afternoon Cody was served a tray of food; spaghetti, barbecue, ice cream, green beans, milk... Wow, what a quick change! Actually he got the wrong tray! He was not supposed to have solid food yet. We had to feed Cody his meal. He was not coordinated enough to feed himself. His appetite wasn't normal, but, after all, he was still in the process of waking up. He didn't eat much and we had to feed him small bites. Cody was weak physically, but he was really trying to cooperate. After eating, Cody asked to brush his teeth. We looked at each other and smiled to think his memory was working! (At home Cody was always faithful about brushing and flossing his teeth on his own every night before bedtime.)

Before the doctors finalized plans to release Cody to the rehabilitation hospital, one more EEG was ordered. This was Cody's fourth one and the third that we were able to personally observe. All the others showed "normal for sleeping'. Ed and Carolyn arrived, so I went out in the hall to wait with them. Ted stayed in the room to be with Cody during the test. We weren't sure if Cody would be still enough for them to perform the procedure and we could hear Cody mumbling something.

As John the technician, was placing the 27 electrodes on his head, Cody looked up at him and asked him, "Do you have Jesus in your heart?" John replied that he did and proceeded with the 'wiring'. Carolyn, Ed and I weren't sure what Cody had said. We heard Cody mumbling something else and then heard very clearly, "…and be filled with the Holy Ghost, in Jesus' name, Amen." I rushed back in to ask Ted what Cody had said, but one look at Ted's face, with tears in his eyes, gave me the answer. Cody wasn't satisfied that John had Jesus in his heart, so Cody prayed for the EEG technician to be filled with the Holy Spirit! **WOW, what anointing coming out of this little man of God.** Just as the technician concluded getting all the electrodes on his head, Cody asked to go to the bathroom. He didn't want to use the urinal; he wanted to go to the bathroom in the bathroom! Ted helped him and guided Cody in the room. That wasn't good enough. Cody asked to have the door shut. Well, his manners were still intact too.

Daddy carried Cody in and laid him down on the bed. Cody lay back down and took a nap as the test was started. We were excited that Cody had such peace and was not scared of all the paraphernalia on his head or of the procedure. This would be a good exam for sure. Once again, Ted told the technician what the test would show just as we told them—"Cody will have a normal EEG showing that he is a healthy boy." Sure enough, the next day the report indicated a normal EEG result.

Dr. Watson stopped by the room to see Cody. She had been such a blessing to us and stayed by his bed so diligently. Changes were coming quickly now. The things we had been praying for were finally happening. Dr. Yetman, the head pediatrician, came by and said they weren't doing Cody much good there at Hermann and reaffirmed the need of rehabilitation. He said that plans were tentative for Cody to be transferred the next day. I had reservations about it, but we had come this far, so we decided to go ahead. The social worker, Peggy Reed, came to talk to us. She began concluding her reports. Staff from TIRR gave us more information on requirements and procedures and they gave us a large notebook about the hospital, along with a list of items Cody would need for his stay there.

The marathon night we had shared together with the busy day were wearing on Ted. He was ready to get back to Texas City. Ed and Carolyn arrived and were poised and ready to stay with Cody until Misty May got there to stay the night. Everything was in place and we both assured Cody we would be back tomorrow. We left about 3:30.

Ted and I quickly left and now we were on our way. As we were exiting the elevator, we met Linda Lofton, a first grade teacher at Cody's school, entering the elevator. She and her son Zachary had come to visit. We quickly described Cody's progress. She shared with us how Cody's story had been shown on a television station in Corpus Christi, Texas, where her sister lived. Many people there had been praying for Cody. It is so encouraging to hear how much people care when a little child is in need. She proceeded upstairs to visit Cody and we headed for Texas City.

As we drove home, the "outside' world seemed so foreign to me. My world had been so condensed for almost two weeks now. The sun seemed so bright; the flowers were waving in the breeze. I had a long list of things to gather and prepare for the new phase that awaited Cody. It was good to be back home, but my heart was with Cody. Brittany had been staying with Grammy and it was refreshing to share some quality time together as a family.

That night after we got Brittany in bed, my mind reviewed the things I needed to get done before returning the next day. I needed to mark Cody's name in all his clothes for the stay at TIRR. They projected his rehabilitation would last four to six weeks. According to their instructions, each piece was to be labeled with a permanent marker. I went through his drawers selecting clothes. I thoroughly enjoyed getting the tennis shoes, clothes, toothbrush and toiletries for him to use. The night was short, relaxation was still in the distance, but our little boy was coming around!

We called the hospital to check on Cody. Carolyn relayed that soon after Ted and I had left the hospital, Cody had pulled the stomach feeding tube completely out! She ran down the hall for the nurse. After reviewing his records and seeing that Cody had eaten some applesauce and food, the doctor's approval was obtained to discontinue the use of the tube. The nurse removed the feeding bag from the IV pole. That was one more line out!

Ed and Carolyn showed Cody home movies, along with a few of his favorite videos. One of his favorite characters was the train Thomas the Tank Engine. They played the music video and the song 'Gone Fishin'!" over and over. Cody sang along and had a good "belly laugh' as he requested them to "Play it again!" That is one way to spend an evening at the hospital! God was doing a work in Cody's brain. Progress was being made. Misty came up after her day at work to spend the remainder of the night with Cody. We knew Cody was in good hands.

Tuesday, July 15th—Day Fourteen

When we returned the next morning, all the IV lines had been removed! Cody was 'unattached' completely! Misty gave us a good report. She told us every detail of the night before. After she relieved Ed and Carolyn, Misty gave Cody a bath and washed his hair. At 9 o'clock, the nurse administered the Methadone and Clonidine. About an hour later, Cody began to get restless. He began seeing bugs and acted like he was climbing a ladder. Misty and Cody held hands and walked the hall about four times to help calm him. Cody was still restless, so Misty requested the Ativan to help him relax. As the medication was given to Cody in the heplock in his arm, Misty noticed that he flinched slightly. After examining the area on his arm, Misty called the nurse and pointed out the redness around the heplock. She suggested to the nurse that it might be a source of obstruction. Soon after her request, the line was removed and Cody was free from all the lines into his body!

Cody had a good evening. He asked for us, but Misty reassured him that we would be back the following morning. She took great care of him. We had total trust and confidence in her to stay with him in our absence. She was a good nurse and understood medical procedures far better than we did.

We appreciated Misty so much. She had called and visited the hospital daily since the fist day of the accident. That was no small task, since she too was a mother and ran her own business.

That night's report was good news. After she shared with us the good news, Misty left to go on to work. Our day was starting out great. This would prove to be our last day at Hermann as a patient. Cody began a soft, mechanical diet and things were progressing. The day was proceeding well and the recovery was "ON"! We started packing and making preparations to go to the next phase of recovery.

We dressed Cody in the short set we brought. It was fun to walk around the floor and greet the staff along the way. It was a joyous time, to say the least. We recognized two of his PICU nurses down the hall. One was Nurse Tracey, a young nurse that took much interest in Cody from the first night. He walked up to her, held out his hand to shake hers, and introduce himself saying, "Hi, I'm Cody Brunt. How are you?" They just looked at Cody in awe. During the afternoon, we watched home movies and watched Cody whistle through the space in his front teeth. It was a new thing he had taught himself while we had been gone. He thoroughly enjoyed his newly acquired skill.

About 5:30 that afternoon, we were officially approved for the transfer to TIRR. I was surprised to hear that an ambulance was coming to transport him. I thought it would be much easier to just load him up in the car and take him over with us. It was hospital policy though and we tried to understand. The ambulance drivers arrived for Cody. They were surprised that he was able to walk. They made the statement, "If we would have known he could walk, we would have used a wheelchair." They had a gurney with them, so they decided to go ahead and use it. Cody was placed on it, laid down, and strapped on. I wanted to go with them, but just like the helicopter, it was not policy for parents to accompany patients during transfers. Ted and I quickly gathered everything on carts, including Cody's great collection of balloons and presents, and hurried to the car. We drove the car around to the street behind Hermann, to the rehabilitation hospital.

We hurried and parked the car and rushed up to the sixth floor. Upon our arrival, we were informed by one of the ambulance drivers that Cody had lost his balance while waiting in the playroom down the hall. He had fallen and hit his head but was all right. Now I really had mixed emotions about being there to begin with, learning about that incident didn't help matters. I knew when Cody had more time to adjust and get all the effects of his drugs out of his system that all would be back to normal.

We were told about the hospital procedures. Cody was only allowed in a wheel chair for transporting him off the floor. He bored quickly with his room, so we'd push him down to the elevator and outside to a courtyard on the ground floor. The outdoors and fresh air was a welcome place, even though it was in the unmerciful July heat. Ted had to leave, in order to get back to Brittany and avoid the evening traffic. Cody and I enjoyed the sun a little longer before returning to the room.

So much had happened in one day, but it felt so good to see things progressing. The doctor in charge of Cody's recovery, Dr. Zidek, talked with me while Cody took a nap. She explained our schedule and estimated our stay at approximately four to six weeks. That was their plan, but we believed God would speed up the recovery time.

We had several visitors that first night at TIRR. Terri Cruse and her daughters came and entertained Cody in the playroom. James and Debbie Benson came later and watched Cody in our "fort". We had a private room and our bed consisted of an air mattress on the floor, surrounded by a three-foot high padded wall on all four sides. It was perfect for Cody and I to stay close together. I called it our "fort" to make it a fun experience for him. It was refreshing to have windows and a view of the outside world: including trees, passing cars, and a skyline.

We had a television right by the bed. For the first time, we could watch our favorite Christian station, TBN. That first night, I played TBN all night to keep the Word in our room's atmosphere. We had an adjoining bathroom. The patients in the next room weren't physically able to use it, so it was like our own private bathroom. I gave Cody a shower as he sat on a shower chair. Everything there was geared for special needs and it was easy to care for Cody. By the time things calmed down, it was after 11:00 p.m. The next day would begin a constant schedule of therapists, but we were ready for the challenges ahead.

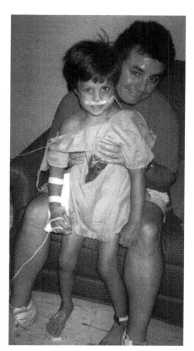

Cody standing up for the first time in our private room with Daddy's support.

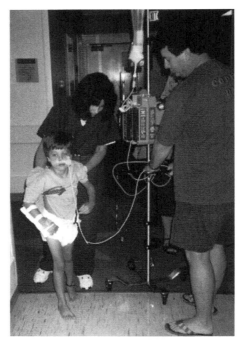

Cody walking for the first time with IV pole & feeding tube 'in tow'.

Chapter 5

Rehabilitation Days...
God is Working
We're Still Standing!

Wednesday, July 16th—Day Fifteen

The rehabilitation schedule was very demanding. We met and had our first sessions with the physical therapists, speech therapists, occupational therapists, and neuro-psychology therapists who would be working with Cody. The hospital gave us a full morning and afternoon schedule. Cody was very cooperative. He stayed calm, even though he didn't understand some of the instructions. It was hard for him to do a series of tasks. I stayed with him during all the sessions except for neuro-therapy; there I took him to the waiting room and the doctor came to take him back into a special testing area. I stayed in the waiting room and read and prayed over Cody's performance and protection. I felt a little uneasy being out of his sight and not knowing all the tests that were administered.

Ted and Brittany came to visit later that afternoon. Cody ate a good dinner. He still needed assistance to eat, but his appetite was improving.

Our two children played basketball in the playroom, down the hall from Cody's room. When we first arrived, Cody couldn't even aim at the goal. In just one day, Cody's agility was improving and his competitive spirit was beginning to show. We put him in the wheelchair and went downstairs to the hospital cafeteria, but it was closed. Cody wanted to go to the gift shop, but it was closed also. Daddy and Brittany left for home. I got some dinner out of a vending machine for myself. I hadn't eaten too much in the last few weeks, because there was too much going on. Here at TIRR, you were not allowed to have food in the room, so the munchies were not an option.

Cousin Edmund was our only visitor this night. Cody sat on Edmund's lap, in a chair at the window, and watched the cars go by outside. Cody enjoyed the action and played a guessing game as to who were in all those vehicles. Edmund helped Cody go to the bathroom. It turned out to be his first bowel movement on a potty. It surprised all of us, but I was glad to see everything returning to normal. I asked Edmund to stay a while longer, so I could get a shower and wash my hair. Tina (his wife) was working late that night anyway, so he was glad to stay a little longer. After Edmund left, I cleaned up Cody and we got ready for bed. The nurse brought in his medications. At least his medicines could be taken orally. Once Cody's head hit the pillow, he was off to la-la-land. That was the first full day of sessions, and while they went well, it was a night to remember.

The medications for the evening were given at about 9:00. We were all cozy in our "fort'. Cody had a blood oxygen indicator wired to his finger. We made a game of it and said it was his "E.T." finger, since it had a red glow light on the tip. He had one at Hermann, so it didn't bother him. Sometime after ten o'clock, the blood pressure monitor alarm began sounding. The nurse would come in, time after time, and reset the machine. I didn't realize something was wrong. I just thought he was turning over and disturbing it. Each time, the nurse would have to come in to reset the machine. After a while, she not only reset the machine but also began to check his eye dilation. It was impossible for me to rest, but Cody was not bothered a bit. He was sleeping well, or so I thought...

Around 12 o'clock, a doctor came in and introduced herself to me as the night doctor, covering for Dr. Zidek. She informed me that Cody's blood pressure was dropping. She had collaborated with Dr. Zidek by phone and requested my permission to put in a "line', just in case Cody needed it later on. What we didn't know at the time was that Cody was given an overdose of Clonidine (blood pressure medicine) and that was the reason for the falling blood pressure. I talked with Cody and explained what the doctor wanted to do. A medical team came in the room to do the procedure in our "fort'. They tried to get a line in Cody's right ankle; then his left ankle. As soon as they inserted the needle, the vein collapsed. The pain and discomfort to Cody was obvious and quite unnerving to me. I was holding him tightly. I snuggled close to his face and whispered to him as they tried rapidly without success. His steady dropping blood pressure was making the alarm go off on the monitor constantly. Things were looking bad again. Cody was unaware of the severity. He was in pain from the repeated needle sticks in both ankles. I told them to stop and let Cody rest a while. The nurse called me to the nurse's station to receive a call from Dr. Zidek. She was calling me from her home. She apologized for the "mistake' and explained the situation, informing me that Cody was approved to return to Hermann if things didn't change soon.

I hung up the phone after talking to the doctor. By this time it was about 2:00 a.m. Could this *really* be happening to us—just when Cody was improving and we were actually making progress? I asked the nurse to get me an outside line to call Ted. I had to inform him of what was going on and to be praying. Ted almost jumped through the phone when I explained the situation. If he hadn't been so many miles away, he would have come up personally and taken things in his own hands. Well, we were miles apart and I had to be the one to handle the situation. He gave me specific questions to ask the doctor, concerning precautions against this ever happening again. I asked him to call Misty and get her suggestions. If he needed to call, I gave him that number since the switchboard is closed to outside lines after hours.

My head was foggy with all the commotion. I returned to the room, and talked with Cody, convincing him to let them try one more time to put in a line. They took us to a treatment room down the hall and tried again. The needle was inserted but the vein collapsed. I told them emphatically, "That's it, don't stick him again. We'll wait it out." I carried Cody back to our room and trusted God to reverse the medication's effects on his blood pressure. God sent a spirit-filled nurse to sit at the end of his bed to pray and intercede with me through the remainder of the night. Cody's blood pressure alarm sounded frequently, but we believed God.

Thursday, July 17th—Day Sixteen

Around 6:30 a.m., the nurse came over to me and said, *"We have another miracle!"* Cody had made it through again! When Cody awakened, he was tired and so was I.

Before 7:00 a.m., a lab nurse came to draw blood. I wasn't thrilled at all for Cody to wake up to that discomfort, so I questioned her about the necessity of the blood tests. I made sure this was not going to become a daily routine. She reassured me that the doctor had ordered it and that it was a one-time procedure. It didn't affect Cody too much, since he was still exhausted from the eventful night.

When he did fully wake up, he woke up hungry! Cody ate slowly, but he wanted to feed himself. He insisted that I put on his shoes and socks first thing. Our schedule that day was lighter. His first session was an hour of physical therapy. Several friends visited from the church: Stephanie Barnes, Christy Martin, and Gina Este. Their children were in vacation Bible school, so they came up to visit. They brought treats and some pictures their children had drawn for Cody. The visit was cut short when the speech therapist came in to get Cody for the next session. I stayed and visited a short while, but my mind was with Cody down the hall. I still didn't feel comfortable with some of the staff being alone with my son, so I excused myself and explained that I needed to be with him. I walked to the therapist's office and sat in on the remainder of the session.

Cody had difficulty reading and writing. In the previous school year he had done well, but this was a "prayer target" to be improved on. During lunchtime, the speech therapist stopped by to watch Cody eat. Cody ate very well and the next step was taken in Cody's diet. The new orders would allow his diet to include chopped foods with bread. The evening meal would be chopped hamburger and potatoes! Cody was still working on his stamina, so he took a rest after lunch.

The afternoon was full of sessions until dinnertime. During the break between sessions, I washed clothes in the laundry room around the corner from our room. I guess the reason why the hospital requested the patient's clothes be labeled was for those patients who didn't have a caregiver. Those clothes could easily get lost in the many loads of laundry.

> **Your child's laughter can do more for you than any medicine; Cody's laughter was certainly helping me.**

By this time, Ted had gone back to work. He had used most of his vacation days. After work that day, Ted called to check on Cody. He and Brittany were not coming to visit that evening; although our friends Roland Kelley and James Benson came for a while. Cody tried to play Nintendo, but his coordination was not improved enough. He was getting frustrated. Ed and Carolyn came to visit for a while as well. One of Cody's favorite things to do there was to shoot hoops in the playroom around the corner. If we weren't in our room, that's where we were. In the previous days it was hard for him to stand and keep his balance, but that evening he was passing the ball and shooting at the basket. His school buddy, Jacob, came to see him, along with Jacob's mother, Teresa Hooter. She took pictures of the boys playing together in the playroom. We sat and thoroughly enjoyed watching the boys play again. Cody was talking better and his sentence structure was improving. Cody got a kick out of saying something and then say, "Made you look!" The four of us sat in a circle on the floor and told "stories'. Cody would try to make up some tales and just begin to laugh…Your child's laughter can do more for you than any medicine; Cody's laughter was certainly helping me. It had been a good day and it ended on a happy note, with friends.

The night medication was delivered. It was to be his last dose of Methadone. All Cody's medications were now administered by two or three nurses and doubled checked to insure the correct dose. Ted had stressed the implementation of a plan that prevented another overdose.

Friday, July 18th, Day Seventeen

Cody awoke refreshed and ate a good breakfast. His blood pressure registered a little low. With the doctor's approval, the therapists were allowed to start our day of sessions. Cody was now allowed to *walk* down to the gym, for physical therapy with Mrs. Rhonda. That day he had a little trouble with the 'gallop', but I knew it would improve. He walked on the balance beam with help. Dr. Zidek told me later, "Cody is making very good progress." She changed her prognosis, from the original 4 to 6-week stay, to a 2-week time frame.

Cody was a fighter and did remarkably well, mastering tasks from one session to the next. So many other children on the floor weren't as physically blessed. Each session presented challenges, but we would pray about them and the next session would bring progress.

I enjoyed reading books to Cody to pass the time. That afternoon before going to work, Cousin Wallace visited and read Cody a story before his occupational therapy session. It was good to see those two together again. Tina came up for a while before she had to go in to work, in downtown Houston. Cody tried again to play the Sega video game, but still had difficulty in maneuvering well. It was time for speech therapy anyway. Later, Al and Hilda Rodefield came and brought him some Hot Wheel toy cars. James Benson and R.C. Colbert, from church, checked in on his progress as well. Cody was tired by dinnertime and he fell asleep shortly after 5 o'clock. He was resting when Daddy, Brittany, and Grammy came in that evening. They brought Wendy's nuggets and french fries with them. It was Cody's favorite meal!

Later that evening, after a hard day of therapy, we had a surprise visit. Cody was involved in his favorite activity—shooting hoops in the playroom. I glanced through the glass window to see Officers Bob and John rounding the corner. They didn't see us, so I stepped out in the hall and invited them in. They were surprised to see Cody standing up. It was their first time to see him awake, out of bed, his eyes open, talking, and walking.

As Cody was shooting baskets, the officers continued to gaze at him. This was the little boy they helped save three weeks ago; now well on the road to recovery! Needless to say, we had a good evening visit. We all went downstairs and the two officers drove their patrol cars up to the entrance doors. Cody got to take a ride with them in the parking lot. Cody and Brittany enjoyed the demonstration of the flashing lights and all of the official "gadgets' in the patrol cars. Ed, Carolyn, and Edmund arrived about that time, to find us "playing' in the parking lot. We all had a good time watching Cody improve and enjoy life. We headed back to the room as the officers went back to work.

Carolyn stayed with Cody that evening and Ted took me home to get some rest. It was Friday and there was no therapy on the weekend, so Saturday would be a rest day. Before leaving, we assured Cody that we'd be back the next day and that Aunt Carolyn would be with him during the night. Cody was beginning to regain his appetite. There was a refrigerator by the nurse's desk with in-between meal treats. Since extra food wasn't allowed in the rooms, we went to the little refrigerator a lot. Carolyn brought a peanut butter sandwich for her snack but it wasn't long until Cody helped himself to it. Up to that point, peanut butter wasn't on his hospital diet, but Cody added it now!

Saturday, July 19th—Eighteenth Day

During the night, Cody asked for Mommy. He slept on and off, but Carolyn sang to him and consoled him as they stayed in "the fort'. Cody was up early at 6:30 a.m. He ate a good breakfast. Edmund and Tina came up around lunchtime to take Carolyn home, but they didn't come empty handed. They brought nuggets and french fries and Cody ate it all! We relieved Carolyn, as she was a little tired from Cody's restless night. We tried to pass the time by watching videos and playing basketball in the playroom. Daddy and Brittany left about 7:30 that evening. The weekends were long, without sessions to attend. Ted and Brittany had hardly gone when Don Stidham and his daughter, Terri Cruse, arrived with some little trucks for Cody. We sat in the room and visited while Cody ate ice cream and played trucks on the bed. Before we knew it, it was time to get cleaned up and get ready for bed. When bedtime came, it was a welcome event for both of us. We snuggled and got cozy in our "fort'.

Sunday, July 20th—Day Eighteen

During the night, Cody was a little restless. He complained of his arm and wrist hurting. The nurse gave him some Tylenol about 4:00 a.m. The morning was bright and sunny as it greeted us through the window. We had arranged with the doctor for a pass for the afternoon. She gave us four hours and we had them all planned. Cody and I got ready for a day with Daddy and Brittany. Cody loved the breakfast with the orange muffin. Ted called on the cellular phone and said he was only five minutes away. I checked Cody out and off we went. The first stop of the day was to the museum, to see the dinosaurs. We arrived only to find out it was closed, so we took a ride on the train at Hermann Park. We drove down to Texas City and stopped by the new house, to show Cody the construction and how his new room was coming along. I was amazed at the progress myself. When we arrived, Beth Cantini was parked in front of the house. She had found out that we had a pass for Sunday and wanted to drop off a few treats for the kids. Among the treats were some colors for Cody's artistic endeavors. Before the accident, he loved to draw dinosaurs. Now it was a major task just to write his name and he had trouble dealing with the imperfection. Cody was previously very meticulous on details.

After our new house visit, we went by Wendy's for lunch, and, of course, Cody ordered chicken nuggets! We had just enough time to stop by the apartment. Brittany had great fun showing all the presents people had given us for Cody. Now he was awake and able to enjoy them and play a while. I gave him a haircut and let him take a bath. He was used to taking baths at home, unlike showers at the hospital. Our four-hour pass was soon running out.

In the parking lot, we were just getting in the car when we heard a honk. We looked up to see our friend, Pat Martin, from church. She jumped out of her car and came over to give Cody a big hug and kiss. As tears welled up in her eyes, it was not hard to see that she was excited to see him up and walking. On the way out of town, we stopped by Roland and Linda Kelley's house. Cody liked playing with their dashound and Linda hadn't seen Cody up and around yet.

On the drive back to the hospital, Cody fell asleep. We arrived at TIRR with no minutes to spare. The four hours had gone by so fast. The Houston Astros were playing on television. Cody is a big baseball fan. We watched the game together, then Daddy and Brittany had to leave and go back home. Cody and I watched their car pull out of the parking lot and we waved to them from the window, trusting that they could see us too. We were up on the sixth floor and Cody commented on how little the car was from our view. Wallace made a quick visit that evening. We had some snacks and enjoyed the pleasant evening. Patti Moore brought some fruit, treats, and "Welcome Back" balloons. She had been out of town and that was the first time she had seen Cody up and awake. It was bedtime again and vital signs were taken at 11:30 p.m.

Monday, July 21st—Day Nineteen

Our first full week of sessions began. Cody woke up strong and ready for breakfast. He ate grapes and cereal. In physical therapy, Cody jumped on a small trampoline; shot hoops, skipped, and did everything he was instructed to do. The therapist released him from using the wheelchair as his only source for transportation. She said that, physically, Cody was doing fine!

The other sessions went well too. Dr. Zidek came for a visit. She inquired how Cody handled Sunday's activities. I had a good report for her and commented that the museum was closed and we weren't able to see the dinosaur exhibit. She wrote my report on his chart and released him to go on an evening pass, on Tuesday, to the museum. The museum of Natural Sciences was just down the street, in Hermann Park. She told me that Cody did not fit into their 'regular' patient recovery pattern. Plans were being made for a Friday dismissal for him. She felt Cody would need additional occupational therapy, but he could do that as an outpatient. He was placed on a regular diet, one that included peanut butter and crackers. Harrold and Helen Osterholm visited between sessions. In the few days of his stay at the hospital, they could see vast improvements in Cody. In speech, and occupational therapy, the staff worked with Cody on writing his name and counting. He increased his whistling skills and began to whistle tunes he would think up. Ted brought up a copy of his school achievement tests and I gave it to the neuro-psychologist that afternoon. Cody tested on their reading tests with a third grade level. Not bad since he would be starting first grade in a month!

After the full day of therapy, Cody wanted to check out the gift shop. We walked down, but again it was closed. We got some candy out of the vending machines and made a date to try again the next day. We went back to the room. Cody needed to go the bathroom, but the phone rang and I had to answer it. Cody went by himself to the bathroom for the first time. Progress! We now had the opportunity to select the meal menu. That evening, Cody had the hospital's chicken strips for dinner. Things were going well. It was a quiet evening with no visitors. We watched videos together, shot hoops in the playroom, and worked with "Legos". After his shower, Cody went to sleep on his own.

Tuesday, July 22nd—Day Twenty

Cody slept better during the night. He was better at eating on his own and he was looking forward to therapy. That day, physical therapy, had different things for us to do. We went outside to a car they had parked in the parking lot. They wanted to see if Cody could open the door, get in, fasten his safety belt, unbuckle it, and get out. We went in a "mock' bathroom and they wanted Cody to get in and out of a bathtub. In the gym, he enjoyed showing the therapists how he could shoot basketball hoops. We even went outside and played a little baseball for the morning session. Cody could still hit the ball pretty far. That day our schedule was a little lighter and went like this:

8:30-9:15 physical therapy
9:30-11:45 neuro-psychological testing
11:00-11:15 speech therapy Lunch
1:00-1:45 occupational therapy
2:30-2:45 speech therapy—excelling
3:00-4:00 neuro-psychology therapy

Dr Zidek came in and discussed Cody being dismissed on Friday, around 1:00 p.m. WOW! We were so excited to finally have a date for him to come home. Cody ate dinner and we waited for Daddy and Brittany to arrive, so we could tell them the good news.

Ted took off from work a little early and arrived with Brittany about 5:30. We quickly headed over to the museum and looked at the dinosaurs. Of course, we had to take another train ride through the park. There was just enough time to drive down the street to eat an order of chicken nuggets, at Wendy's, and arrive back by 8:00. This outing was a highlight to the day's activities.

When we arrived back at TIRR, we were informed there was a new patient coming in and the hospital needed Cody's room. His room had been right in front of the nurse's station. Uncle Ed, Aunt Carolyn, and Geneva were already waiting on us. We had to empty the room completely. We all picked up a suitcase, gathered the balloons, took down pictures and cards off the wall, carried flower arrangements, etc. We packed up Cody's stuff and moved everything down to room 605. He would have a roommate now. We had met Mercedes and his parents on our first day there. This little boy had an accident in June. He had been riding his bike and was hit by a car. Mercedes had a head injury that paralyzed his arm and leg, but he was coming along well. His parents both worked during the day, so he was glad to have a roommate. Both Cody and Mercedes had "forts' as beds. They were both about the same age too.

We all visited for a while before everyone had to leave. I gave Cody a shower, trying to slow down the pace after a busy day. While I was washing and rinsing his hair, I found a big bald spot in the back of Cody's head. I tried to stay calm, but as soon as I got him dried off and back in the room, I headed for the nurse. She examined the spot and assured me it was only a 'pressure' area, from laying on the bed so long in PICU, and the hair would grow back. I was concerned that his hair was falling out! What a relief to know that "this too shall pass". Looking at Cody that day, you could not tell that, less than a month earlier, he had been in an accident. There were only a few needle marks on his body and one small burn mark on his chest (probably made from the metal monitor tabs).

Wednesday, July 23rd—Day Twenty-one

Again, Cody slept well. After breakfast, he started physical therapy with Mrs. Rhonda. She was explaining various exercises to work on as she completed the discharge test papers. Speech therapy followed, with Dr. Jay. Cody had really come a long way. I commented on how Cody's eyes were still dilated and questioned if this was normal. Dr. Jay made a notation of my comment and promised to discuss it later.

Cody loved to watch the TV program "Arthur", so, immediately after speech, we rushed back to the room to watch his favorite program. Dr. Zidek came in and discussed Cody's progress and discharge plans. It was lunchtime and

Cody was ready to eat. After lunch, Cody took his regular nap. (He quit taking naps by the time he was three years old.) Now, his body was still in the healing process and needed extra rest.

The afternoon was very busy. A favorite activity for Cody was when "Callie", the hospital cat, came to visit. Some of the volunteer girls knew how much Cody liked pets, so in their spare time, they'd go get Callie and bring her up for a visit. This afternoon, we were able to have AAT therapy. They had this activity on the third floor. Volunteers from the community brought their pets and the patients were able to touch and pet them. Research indicated that this was a therapy that worked well on brain injured patients.

Ted called that evening and talked with Cody on the phone. I was informed that the hospital had an annual outing for patients to the circus. They asked me if Ted and Brittany could come too, so I asked Ted over the phone that night. We made plans to all go to the circus the following Thursday evening. I anticipated a great family-fun day at the circus. Our children had never gone to a big circus and they were all excited. Cody and I would have to ride in the hospital van, but Ted could follow behind in the car with Brittany.

Misty and Joshua May came to visit after dinner. Misty brought me a meal from the nearby Luby's cafeteria. I hadn't realized how little I had been eating. Joshua and Cody shot hoops in the playroom while we visited and had an evening of leisure. During the night, Cody's wrist and hand hurt again. We prayed over it. I looked at the outside and it didn't have any marks or anything to indicate what was causing the pain. Each time the pain woke Cody up we prayed, then he could settle back down and go off to sleep without needing medication.

> **We were still standing and not compromising our belief for a complete comeback.**

Thursday, July 24th—Day Twenty-two

The days in rehab had been rewarding, but there was a new focus coming into view...DISCHARGE! Cody was sleeping better through the night and the daily schedule was changing to make plans for final testing. I requested to sit in on the doctor's weekly team meeting, as they evaluated each of the patient's progress and goals.

Our room was very busy, with hospital staff checking on us and making appropriate accommodations. One of the doctor's target concerns was Cody's eye/brain perception. That afternoon Cody had an eye examination. The results were 'far sightedness', explaining his visual problems with reading. One of the doctors shared with me that Cody had made tremendous progress. I loved to get those reports. We were confident that, in time, Cody's healing would be complete. We were still standing and not compromising our belief for a complete comeback.

> **Philippians 1:6—Jesus will complete the work He started in Cody!**

Through out the afternoon, the various tests continued. Cody was working hard with each doctor. The hospital was in the process of notifying his school, concerning his educational needs. Arrangements were being made for some outpatient therapy, at a location as close to our home as possible. They wanted a facility that catered to small children.

I made sure Cody was situated in his room and made arrangements to be at the doctor's conference that afternoon, as my request had been granted to attend the weekly meeting. My notebook and questions were prepared. I was eager to hear from each of the doctors about their concerns and Cody's progress. As I listened, I could sense their admiration for our little trooper. Cody was very cooperative, even though he couldn't understand their directions at times. One doctor looked at me and said,

> **"Less than one percent of patients that were in Cody's condition ever fully recover."**

That night, we were all looking forward to going to the circus as a family. It would be Cody and Brittany's first circus. After dinner, Ted and Brittany arrived and we were all ready to go on a big "fling', as this was our last night at the hospital. Cody and I had to go in the hospital handicap van, with the other patients, but Brittany and Dad followed us to the Summit. The directors had pre-arranged to pick up the tickets at the ticket window.

Somehow in the shuffle, Ted was not allowed to park the car with us and we got separated. One of the therapists took Cody in to watch the show while I stood around for an hour at the entrance waiting on Brittany and Ted. I didn't know that they were on the other side of the building waiting for us! By the time I thought about looking at the other entrance, they had given up and driven back to Texas City. I was so disappointed.

Inside, Cody had too much to look at, with three rings of activities going on at one time. My mind was racing, not understanding why I couldn't find Brittany and Ted. Our group of patients all sat together. A few of the patients had their family members there as well. Two patients were on ventilators and had a personal therapist escorting them. It was a pleasant evening of entertainment. As I looked at the severity of some of the patients, some were in wheelchairs and others were on portable ventilators, I was overwhelmed with gratitude to God for the blessings He had given us.

On the ride back to the hospital, I sat with Cody asleep and buckled into the seat next to me. Tears of joy began to trickle down my face as the culmination of the last three weeks began to impact my emotions. We had watched a miracle take place. The entire time I had resisted the temptation to break down and become consumed by the overwhelming obstacles that we faced. That struggle seemed almost a distant memory. As we went back to the hospital, the atmosphere in the van was very quiet. Most of the children were asleep. The circus excitement was so different from their usual routine. We arrived back at the hospital a little before ten o'clock. All the patients were unloaded and we rode the elevator up to the room. We quickly got cleaned up and ready for our last night in the hospital. Events of the past three weeks were finally registering with me. God had been so very good to us. He had given Cody a new brain and new lungs. We were about to begin another chapter in Cody's recovery story.

Friday, July 25th—Day Twenty-three

DISCHARGE DAY!

Cody was so easy going during our final day in the hospital. He didn't realize the monumental progress he had made. Peace covered him, like a blanket, throughout the whole experience. After breakfast, we had our final physical therapy session. We were able to say our "good-byes" and truly express our gratitude for the fine job each therapist had done with our son.

The hospital's administrator, Marisa Hurst, phoned me in the room. She said that a newsperson from Houston's CBS affiliate, Channel 11 News, called to see if we would do an interview before we left the hospital. My friend, Regina Nilsson, told me she was going to call the station and give them the first chance for an interview. I guess she really followed through with her plan. Regina said, "The station reported the bad news, now lets let them report the good news." Sure enough, she had called and Channel 11 accepted her offer. The news station wanted to do a follow-up story on "Cody's Comeback". The hospital approved and the interview was scheduled for one o'clock. Ted and Brittany came up at about eleven and we started packing all our stuff. We gave away a lot of Cody's balloons to his patient-friends.

The news crew arrived right on time and was escorted to our room by the hospital's public relations director, Nancy Hutchins. Excitement filled the air, the lights went on and the camera began rolling. Health reporter, Susan Starnes, conducted the interview. I was not able to really comprehend the severity of Cody's accident at this time and people who had more experience with this type of situation were amazed at Cody's recovery. The interview went well. Afterwards, we chatted with Susan for a while. At that point, I began to believe God wanted this story to be told "around the world'. This was only the start of a great testimony of God's healing power on the earth today.

> **...I began to believe God wanted this story be told 'around the world'.**

Cody was getting excited to be able to go home and get on with his life. On the way out, Mrs. Hutchins asked us to pray with a little one year-old boy, who was also a near-drowning victim. He was on a ventilator, fighting for his life, and his mom was by his bed. We tried to explain our testimony to her, but she didn't speak English and our Spanish was limited. Love and compassion have no communication barriers, so we prayed and loved the both of them and believed God to give comfort and healing.

After eleven days at TIRR, and thirteen previous days at Hermann, we were finally on our way HOME! It wouldn't be complete without a last stop over to Hermann, to visit the PICU staff that had taken such good care of Cody. We rode the elevator up to the sixth floor and entered the PICU. It was so much fun to go in with Cody and watch him introduce himself to his caregivers. Of course, I was catching this great moment on film. Ted and I stood tall as the proud parents of such a sweet boy. The doctors just looked in awe at Cody's agility and recovery.

We stopped by the Life Flight office. Nurse Lynn Ethridge, one of the helicopter nurses, explained to us that on the day of the accident they were on a return trip from Galveston. The aircraft was in close proximity to Clear Lake and it really expedited serious lifesaving time.

This scene was just like we proclaimed to the hospital staff three weeks before:

> **Cody will walk out of this hospital 100 percent restored, just like in the picture!**

We did not back off of our confession. We had spoken faith-filled words. We guarded the words Cody heard during his recovery. God's plan worked!

On our way driving into town, our first stop was to the church office to see if our pastor was in. It was like a reunion for the staff to see the miracle we all had prayed for actually walk in and greet them. We drove around the building to the school office. Joy flooded our hearts to realize in less than a month, Cody would be re-entering these doors as a first grade student.

The day was not over. We stopped by the new house and showed Cody his room and looked over the progress. We stopped by Misty May's house. She had a big surprise for Cody. (While Cody was in a coma, she had told him when he woke up she would buy him a go-cart.) Well, she had done her shopping and there it was, waiting in her driveway, ready for Cody to hop on and ride away. We had some other stops to make and made arrangements to ride later that evening. We had ice cream at Baskin-Robbins and came home to the apartment. Cody was enjoying his many gifts. Now it was time to play!

That evening we watched the television interview on the CBS affiliate, KHOU-11 in Houston. After seeing the original footage of the accident for the first time, I was amazed at the news coverage. The interview was very well done and expressed our appreciation to all that had prayed for us during this time. We had a miracle and were glad to tell the world about it.

After watching the television interview together as a family, Brittany and Cody went to play in the bedroom while Ted and I remained on the couch. We couldn't help but overhear Cody and Brittany talking about the news report. Cody was bragging about his underwater skills, "Yea Brittany, I held my breath for seven minutes!" There was a pause and Brittany proceeded to explain her version. She said emphatically, *"Cody, you were dead...You were graveyard dead. The only difference between you and Lazarus was that you didn't stink!"*

We couldn't help but chuckle to ourselves. Up to that point, Ted and I had been careful to gently tell Cody that he had been under the water for a long time, that he had breathed water instead of air, and had been very sick. We explained that he had been "asleep' for a long time. It was an easy way of explaining to him about the accident without putting too much on him. We did not want him to have flashbacks or fear of any kind. Brittany just cut through the fluff and got down to the nitty-gritty with him. Kids are like that. It was our first evening all together in the apartment in almost a month. It was good just to be healthy together again.

Sunday, July 27th

What a wonderful day! We dressed and got ready to enjoy a great time in church. As we arrived, so many friends met us and shared their love. During the service, pastor called us to the platform. The church roared with enthusiasm. God had truly answered prayers and brought life back into our son. Pastor asked Cody if he had anything to say. Cody stood in front of a crowd of over 2,000 people and made one comment that sums up the whole story:

"GOD ALWAYS WINS!"

It was truly a victory celebrating time. *The church you belong to can mean life or death to you.* We are very privileged to be in an active New Testament church. We had a vast network of loving friends that prayed, loved, called, visited, and brought meals. Churches all over the area were praying with us too; so many we didn't even know.

The church you belong to can mean life or death to you.

After the service, a man walked up to Ted and I and asked me if we recognized him. I looked and honestly said "no". He went on to introduce himself as Dan Darnell, "the man with the boat". Wow, this was the man that towed Wallace's sailboat and then came and helped us at the scene of the accident. It was a joy to meet him and his family that day. We came to find out that he attends our church.

Thursday, July 30th

Cody began to write his name and color, with some help. Cody was very meticulous in his writing before the accident and it was a little frustrating for him to not be able to do the skills he had previously done well. He was improving with each day. We encouraged him to stay with it, knowing he would do all the things he could do before the accident with even better skill.

Friday, July 31st

Cody had a "date' with his K-5 teacher, Mrs. Benson. The trip had been postponed after school was out, then Cody's accident happened. She wanted to be sure that Cody was well enough to make it. This trip was the reward for winning the top reader award. He had the privilege of choosing the place he wanted to eat lunch. Dessert was to be ice cream at Baskin Robbins. He selected lunch at Wendy's and the menu of chicken nuggets and french fries. It was a little strange to see our son loading up in a car and driving away after all the things that had happened in the last month. The luncheon was a fun time and Cody enjoyed his "date' with his teacher.

The first week in August

Cody began swimming again, in less than a week of being released from the hospital. On Tuesday, August 5, 1997, Cody's comeback story made the front page of the Galveston

Daily Newspaper. The next day, I received a phone call from reporter Phil Archer, of the NBC affiliate in Houston, KPRC Channel-2. He saw the newspaper write up and wanted to come down and do a personal interview. I was surprised at the news coverage and was glad to tell this miracle story every opportunity I got. Phil and a cameraman came to the apartment that afternoon. When I told him Cody was swimming, he suggested that we go down to the pool and shoot the story.

We sat by the pool as Cody and Brittany swam. It was a very casual setting and Phil seemed to be well versed in the magnitude of this miracle. His wife was a medical helicopter nurse and he knew more medical terms than I did. He had done many reports on accident victims that hadn't recovered. I could sense his pleasure in doing this report.

I wasn't sure when the camera was on or off, so we just talked and enjoyed watching the little miracle in motion. Cody swam like a fish, holding his breath and diving under the water. He had no fear of the water, no remembrance of the tragedy, and no nightmares, just like we had prayed.

Cody's remarkable recovery was Channel 2's lead story that afternoon, on the news at 4:00. The show opened with me making the statement, *"Jesus raised people from the dead in the Bible and, if He did it for them, I figured He'd do it for us."* They did a great presentation, in which God got the credit. We were also able to express our appreciation to all those who prayed with us in receiving this miracle.

Saturday, August 16th

The Koneman family gave Cody a swimming party at their home, to celebrate his 'comeback'.

Every miracle needs a Victory Celebration!

Many of Cody's friends came and helped celebrate the
goodness of God. We usually spent the fourth of July at the
Koneman's, so this was a delayed "liberty celebration".

In the weeks to follow...

We took Cody to several outpatient occupational therapy
sessions in Baytown. At the first session, I could see
improvements between the exit exams from TIRR and their
entrance exams on Cody. His eye-hand coordination had
improved, in that short time. His vision cleared up and he
began seeing and reading just fine. There were giant leaps of
improvement with each session and Cody quickly achieved
their goals.

Monday, August 18th

Cody started school August the 18th; right on time, right on
grade level. Our pastor stated to us later that he had a watchful
eye on our car as we drove onto the parking lot that morning.
He watched as Cody walked into the registration line.

The therapists at TIRR had notified his teacher and principal
of Cody's "needs', what things to watch for, and how to help
and assist him. Melanie Alexander, the school nurse, was
quick to place Cody under her wing. It became evident very
soon that God was *"perfecting those things which concerned
us."*

During the weeks following the accident, we found out
more and more how God had everything in control on the day
of the accident. God had specific people in a position to assist
us and help in the rescue of our son.

> **What the devil meant for evil, God turned it around and made Tragedy become a victory!**

Saturday, October 11th

By this time, our new home was completed and we had moved in. We combined an "Open House" and a "Welcome Back Cody" party into one event. The medical staff at the hospitals and those that helped in the rescue had all been invited, but the weather did not cooperate. There was a flash-flood warning in Houston and it rained all day. The weather hindered many out-of-town friends from coming, but we had the party anyway. Ed had one hundred tee shirts printed up that had **"Praise God for Cody Brunt's Miracle"** with the date of the accident on the front. On the back, they had the words to the song **"Look What the Lord has Done"** personalized with Cody's name in it and a little dinosaur on the end. That had been the theme song we sang every night after we prayed together at the hospital. We gave away the shirts to each family that came, for them to "wear and tell' the story of God's miracle working power. We had a good time all day long, from ten o'clock that morning until after nine that night. It was an all-day celebration!

Spring and Summer, 1998

During the spring T-ball season, Cody was the leading home run hitter on his team. The coach used him at first and third base and as pitcher. At the end of the season, he was selected to play third base (*the hot corner*) on the all-star team. For the second year, both Cody and Brittany participated in the city's summer track program. This time Cody wanted to enter some running events and did well. The previous year he had only participated in field events. He won several ribbons and was looking forward to the next summer and possibly qualifying for the state track meet. For his seventh birthday, March 18th, he had a big party at our home. We invited both first grade classes. Officer Bob and his girlfriend attended and marveled at Cody's continuous physical and mental progress. Cody had a good year in the first grade. Every semester his grades improved. At the end of school, during the awards night in May, Cody was awarded the A-B Honor roll certificate and a medal for the highest reader in his class. In June, I went with both children, and a group from our church, to a summer camp. Country Camp is a large facility in Columbus, Texas where some precious friends, Tommy and Rachel Burchfield, host thousands of campers each summer. Rachel has been a friend for many years and had called me at the hospital when Cody was so critical. She prayed with me and told me the campers would be praying too. Now it was our joy to actually attend the camp and share Cody's testimony. Some of the staff remembered praying for our son and rejoiced with us on his miraculous recovery. For our family summer vacation, we went to a large water park, Schlitterbahn, in New Braunfels. Cody rode all the "wild and crazy' rides, some of which he was barely tall enough to ride. We "lived' in the water for several days. The rapids and fast currents didn't phase him. Cody has absolutely no fear of water and has had no nightmares about the accident, just like we prayed.

Fall and Winter, 1998

During the first month of school, in September, I was going over a Bible lesson with Cody at the kitchen table. On the paper was a picture of Jesus in a robe. He casually commented to me, "Mom, I saw Jesus." I tried to stay calm and collected. We had encouraged Cody to be sure and tell us when he remembered anything about the accident. Up to this point, he had not talked about it at all. Cody continued to say, "I saw a bright light and

Jesus walked out of that light. He came up to me and said some words, but I can't remember them right now." I assured him that it was all right that he didn't remember the words Jesus spoke to him but someday he would remember. When Ted got home from work that evening, I asked Cody to repeat his story. The story didn't alter any; Cody said it so matter-of-factly. During the Christmas holidays, Ted and Cody were walking through the mall. They walked by a Christian bookstore that had some kind of display poster in the window. Cody glanced at the drawing and asked Ted if that was Jesus. Ted said that it was an artist's rendition of Jesus. Cody casually remarked, "He doesn't look like that." and walked on. Maybe someday he will be able to share all of what he saw. I am convinced that Cody went to heaven during the time he drowned. During that period of time, Cody was able to see things only those who have been to heaven see. I also believe the words Jesus was speaking to him were something like, "Cody, I know you like it here, but your Mother is calling My name and calling you back to earth, you'll have to go now..." Someday we will know for sure just what their conversation consisted of. Recently, I heard Brother Kenneth E Hagin Sr. share his testimony concerning his death experience as a teenage boy. He mentioned that he could not talk about it for twenty-five years. He said it was so sacred. I finally understand why Cody isn't free to discuss his heavenly visit. His vocabulary can't express it and it is too sacred to talk about. Maybe some day he can.

At the printing of this book, Cody has just completed the second grade. He was on the Honor Roll, each semester, and maintained an A+ average of 98. He was presented the Highest Academic Award in his class and a Perfect Attendance medal. He continues to excel in everything he puts his hand to. Cody played PeeWee baseball and made the league's All Star team as well. The Lord has perfected all of Cody's physical and mental abilities.

God does hear our prayers, as they are in line with His Word. God will do *anything* you can find in the Word and believe Him for. God is so faithful to His Word if we'll just trust Him and believe Him.

NOTHING IS IMPOSSIBLE WITH GOD!
ABSOLUTELY NOTHING!

Brittany & Cody in his 'fort' at TIRR.

23 days after the accident—Dismissal from TIRR.

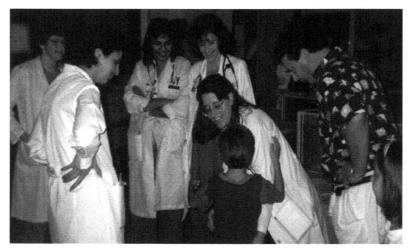

**Returning to Hermann PICU; shaking hands with the
doctors who cared for him.**

First church service with Pastor. Cody with microphone saying, "GOD ALWAYS WINS!"

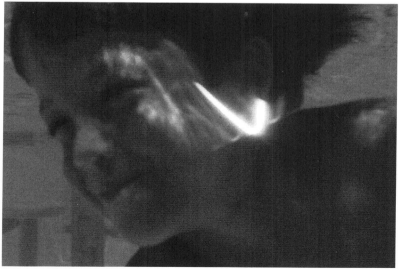

Cody swimming under water and enjoying it!

Cody at 9 years old at time of first printing 2000

Chapter 6

And the child grew...

"And the child grew, and waxed strong in spirit, filled with wisdom: and the grace of God was upon him." **Luke 2:40**

This scripture describes how Cody has continued to grow physically and in his spiritual walk with the Lord. The first printing of this book was released in 2000. I was given an opportunity to bring Cody's life up-to-date, so this chapter 6 is written to show how the miracle continues. Please don't take it as a chapter of a bragging mother. In the years after Cody's miraculous recovery, we saw just how wonderful the new brain and new lungs the Lord restored him with. What the medical profession could not do—our Heavenly Father provided in abundance. We had a big change in the education of both our children when they repeatedly asked to be home schooled. Since I have a teaching degree and Master's degree in Educational Management, I agreed—only after much prayer and planning. I found a local support group and we began home schooling when Cody was in the 3rd grade and Brittany was in the 5th grade.

We were in the classroom one morning and I asked the children if they liked home school. Cody's answer surprised me. He said, "Mom I like home schooling because I don't have to wait for other kids to get finished before we go to the next part of the lessons." I realized that Cody and Brittany can go at their pace and utilize the time in the classroom and not just have a lot of "busy work" to take up the time. The first year Cody completed two years of math since he could go at his own pace. We gave them scholastic achievement tests to make sure they were on grade-level courses. It was a lot of work, but the benefits were worth it all. So, for the next five years we home schooled our children and saw they blossom in personalized Christian curriculum, field trips and various activities including college classes at our local community college under the umbrella of the home school support group. We raised our children to be protected and insulated but not isolated from the 'secular' world, so by the time they reached the 9th grades, we placed them in public school. They entered the high school above average academically, so they qualified to be in advanced classes. Both Brittany and Cody excelled in athletics as well as academics. In Cody's freshman year, he began on the JV baseball team and ended the season on the varsity team. Both Brittany and Cody played varsity tennis and both were 4 year lettermen in the sport.

During Cody's high school years, he worked a part-time job at a local clothing store. He learned customer appreciation and valuable people skills that he uses to this day. Cody is the life of the party wherever he is. He has a repertoire of various movie character impersonations and is almost a stand-up comedian. The Children's minister at church invited him to help out in the children's department. He has a heart to be around children and see how they absorb the Word of God and are so tender toward the things of God. He worked with the children for about five years and now works with the youth group at church. He ministers the offerings and helps out with crowd control and lessons. Cody has a very caring and compassionate personality that transcends the ages from young children to the elderly. Cody learned at a young age that is very important to give back and not just be a "taker" in life's journey.

When Cody was in the 11th grade, he started pursuing a career in the health care profession. He took a class—Health, Science & Technology that was the springboard from what he does today. He had a true desire to be in hospitals and help people. During our discussion one day, I told him that hospitals are definitely a "mission field" of hurting people. His teacher arranged for him to go two days a week for several hours and observe in various department rotations at our local hospital. This was a very valuable program that gave him the opportunity to experience the various departments and their demands and requirements. Through this program he became very interested in the radiology department and the various modalities available in that area of health care.

Cody was accepted to be in "Collegiate High School" program for his senior year of high school. He took all college classes at the community college campus his senior year of high school, and got college credit for those courses. One of his instructors arranged for him to go to Galveston to the huge UTMB medical center to do clinical rotations in the Radiology department. His desire continued to grow in the health profession with this course of study, he was well on course to pursue his future career. In 2008 Cody graduated high school and ranked 12th in his graduating class with many honors and scholarships. To God be all the glory—what a l-o-n-g way Cody had come from being declared having "irreversible brain damage" to these high academic achievements. The Lord continued to guide Cody with every step of his higher education journey.

Cody actually began his college studies while in his senior high school year. So when he started on the Galveston College campus, it was a continuation to pursue an Associate degree in Applied Science in Radiography degree in two years. He earned his certification as an x-ray technician but continued an additional year to get his CT and MRI certifications. He began working at our local hospital in the Radiology department in 2010. While working at the local hospital, Cody continued to work on his bachelor degree at the University of Texas at M. D. Anderson Cancer Center in Houston. He achieved his Bachelor of Science in Diagnostic Imaging degree in three semesters and graduated Summa Cum Laude...now that's a testimony of the goodness of God and how only HE can change situations around for His glory!!!

At the time of this book's second printing, Cody will complete his Master's of Business Administration in Health Care Management degree by November 2014. His desire is to be in charge of a radiology department and continue to help people.

2013 presented Cody several opportunities to share in churches and various venues, the experience and things he saw when he went to heaven during his death experience as a six year old boy. After all these years, this experience has been inside him, but just recently the time has come for him to share with the world the joys of heaven and what awaits Christians as their final destination. We knew that when the Lord was ready for Cody to share his testimony—HE would open the doors. We believe that opportunities will continue to be given to Cody to share his miraculous testimony. Cody has always had a desire to return to heaven because of the awesome sights and extraordinary experience. He knows the time we spend on earth is only a small time period compared the greatness of eternity. The things that he saw and experienced in heaven imprinted his life and a Divine longing to return has never left him.

One afternoon this past year, Ted, Cody and I had an interesting discussion sitting around our breakfast table. Cody said something that really took me back. We were discussing several aspects of the accident and for a rare time, Cody spoke freely and candidly about his account of what actually happened. I was relating my personal viewpoint, experience and what Ted and I were living out that first night at the hospital. The doctors gave us the diagnosis that Cody had irreversible brain damage due to the lack of oxygen and the continued extremely low oxygen levels as well as his lungs being full of water. So many emotions stole my sleep. When I'd try to close my eyes to get some sleep, I was tormented with the scene of Cody struggling in the darkness under the boat running out of air and drowning. As our conversation continued, Cody calmly explained how it really was under the boat and just exactly how he felt throughout the drowning experience. As he described being in the dark, tangled up in the ropes and unable to swim to the surface of the water. As he elaborated how he was unable to hold his breath any longer, he said very calmly, "Mom it didn't hurt". I said "What do you mean Cody, '*It didn't hurt.*'?" He described that when he couldn't hold his breath any longer and had to breathe in the water, things went silent and dark. He let us know that death did not hurt. How profound. Most people fear death and the unknown, but Cody very emphatically said "It doesn't, hurt...

death doesn't hurt." At that moment I really can't explain how relieved I was to know Cody wasn't alone, helpless and scared during his last moments under the boat that day. I told Cody he really needed to include that piece of information every time he shares his testimony. As Christians, we do not need to fear death. When it is our time to leave this world, we will just move to a new address and crossing out of this world to heaven...doesn't hurt!!!

Cody knows that the Lord has a plan and purpose for him to complete. That's why Cody was unable to stay in heaven as a six year old. The Lord told him he had to go back, that his time to go to heaven was not yet. He could not stay in heaven because he had more things to accomplish on earth. Today, Cody is endeavoring to take advantage of each opportunity to share how good God is. As you read this book, you need to realize God has a plan and purpose for your life as well. There is no better feeling than to know you are in the right place, at the right time, with the right people, doing the right thing fulfilling your God-given destiny. Continue to *"...grow in grace, and in the knowledge of our Lord and Savior Jesus Christ. To Him be glory both now and for ever. Amen."* II Peter 3:18.

Conclusion

As we look back over the miracle recovery of our son, we agree with the Word that *"Jesus Christ is truly the same yesterday, today and forever." (Hebrews 13:8)* God's Word is Truth *and the Word of God WILL work for you every time. I mean every time!* His Word is powerful and He has given His Word for us to overcome in every situation. **When we put God's Word in our mouths and speak it out in faith, we will see results. Our pastor says it like this, "If you say what God says, for the same reason God says it, you will get God's results." Mark 11:23-24 lets us know how important the words we say are.** *"And Jesus replying said to them, "Have faith in God (constantly) Truly, I tell you, whoever says to this mountain, be lifted up and thrown into the sea! And does not doubt at all in his heart, but believes that what he says will take place, it will be done for him. For this reason I am telling you, whatever you ask for in prayer, believe—trust and be confident—that it is granted to you, and you will (get it)."* (Amp) In this passage, Jesus puts the emphasis on saying and believing.

To receive our son back to life was not a "cake walk'. It was not easy. It didn't happen instantaneously, but God did give us our miracle. The Bible tells us that we fight the "good fight' of faith (I Timothy 6:12). It's a good fight because we always win in God!

I can remember my quiet times of reading, praying, and studying the Word. The devil would come and say that I was wasting my time and that I could be doing other things. I'm so glad I made the time to have a relationship and fellowship with my Heavenly Father.

Several scriptures that we stood on were:

Isaiah 54:17 *"No weapon that is formed against you shall prosper..."*

Isaiah 55:11 *"So shall My word be that goes forth out of My mouth; it shall not return to Me void—without producing any effect, useless—but it shall accomplish that which I please and purpose, and it shall prosper in the thing for which I sent it."*

Isaiah 57:19 *"...I create the fruit of his lips and I will heal him..."*

Preparation time is never wasted time. I heard Joyce Meyer say, "If you put the Word of God in your heart when you don't need it, you will have it when you do need it." That is so true and you must be diligent to prepare yourself spiritually at all times.

"The people that do know their God are strong and do exploits!"
according to Daniel 11:32.

We live in a time when the devil is deceiving those that can be deceived. I'm determined to know God in such a way that immediately I can perceive when the enemy is trying to get me off track.

Preparation time is never wasted time.

Yes, bad things happen to good people and attacks will come. We need to know that God is a good God and the devil is a bad devil. If tragedy comes to you, don't blame God. The devil comes to kill, steal, and destroy. That is his job (John 10:10). Our Heavenly Father loves us and will bring us help in every area of our lives. He gives us guidelines and instructions to follow in His Word. It is *our* responsibility to know what is rightfully ours and use the Word of God to be victorious. God's Word works!

The church you belong to can be life or death to you.

I stated earlier that 'the church you belong to could be life or death to you'. We learned this from evangelist Ed Dufresne, when he came to our church and spoke that powerful word. It is vitally important to be part of a Bible believing church, where the Word of God is preached. God promises protection to those firmly planted in a New Testament church today. The church is 'a spiritual covering' for your family. We can say from experience that this is true. If your church doesn't believe in miracles, you probably won't receive one. Our family has made a decision to be right in the middle of what God is doing in the earth today.

If you have never made Jesus Christ the Lord of your life, you can do so now. The Bible assures us that we can know for certain that we will spend eternity in heaven, by accepting the price that Jesus paid for us. Romans 10:9-10 gives us the simple plan. You can pray this right now, make heaven your eternal destiny, and have the Lord help you in every situation. Pray this out loud with me:

"Father, I come to you in Jesus' name. I believe Jesus is your Son. I believe in my heart and confess with my mouth that Jesus is Lord and I invite Him to be Lord of my life today. I believe that Jesus came to earth, was born, lived, died, and rose again. He took the penalty of my sins. Father, forgive me of all my sins and cover them with the blood of Jesus. I now

*receive Jesus as the Lord of my life. Thank you for saving me.
I am born-again and I will live with you forever. Amen."*

We give God all the glory and praise for bringing Cody back to life and totally restoring him to health in every physical, spiritual, and mental area. I can truly say today that God answers prayers of faith and will perform His Word for all that believe.

I have come to the conclusion that one of the main problems for Believers is not so much our 'faith' or lack of it. The Word says we only need 'mustard size' faith to get things. (Faith is a product of our spirit. Doubt and Unbelief are products of the mind.) I believe our real problem is Unbelief. We try to reason things out, but all God instructs us to do is Believe. Jesus addressed this subject when the disciples could not heal a boy possessed by a demon in Matthew 17:14-21. Jesus was referring to 'unbelief' that will come out by prayer and fasting. For far too long, people have interpreted that story to say this big miracle had to have prayer and fasting to see it come to pass, but the subject was 'unbelief'.

I encourage you to believe and trust God for whatever you need. He loves you so much!

May God bless you and may He bring faith and hope to you...

Epilogue

During Cody's miracle, so many friends and family surrounded us with prayer, love, phone calls, and much needed support. It would be impossible to make a list of each individual that made this miracle possible. We are so appreciative of all those who prayed and stood with us. Words are inadequate to express how much it meant to us.

I have asked several people, who were involved with this incident, to give a brief excerpt of the miracle from their perspective. May this bring added insight to you concerning this life-changing event.

*****

"The revelation demonstrated with Cody Brunt's miracle is of God's great love for us, His creation, and what He'll do for us if we trust in Him and allow Him to bless us His way. I don't remember how I first heard of the drowning accident, but my wife Marvia and I started praying immediately. We felt compelled to go to the hospital. As a physician, I know how important it is to be specific in a patient's needs (Matthew 7:7-11). I purposed to identify the specific medical needs, obtained from his attending physicians, for Cody's body and brain and petitioned God for them. His physician gave us hope that Cody might live, but if he did, it would probably be in a vegetative state—institutionalized. While in ICU we laid hands on him praying for each organ system that was challenged.

There was no doubt the Brunt family was in intense spiritual warfare. They, like everyone, still had to recognized the facts; Cody drowned, he was pronounced dead, he went to the ICU, required extensive medical intervention, his organ systems were severely damaged, and they would need to fight for his life. However, God, in His mercy through medicine (a gift of God to all mankind, even to those who hate Him) kept Cody on earth's timeline until the ministering angels delivered the answers Cody's parents were asking for. They knew the facts were subject to change by the truth. The truth is the Word of God. They stood on the truth, expecting the facts to change and they did.

Cody's ordeal glorifies and testifies to God's mercy, love, power, presence, and responsiveness through our Lord, Jesus Christ. We also see in this crisis the need to know the Word of God and have it stored in our heart. We do know that what Satan meant for evil and destruction has turned, once again, to God's glory."

Richard Walker, M.D.—Ella's OB-GYN at the time Cody was born.

*****

"Ted, on July 2, 1997, I observed you demonstrate the Christian principle of making a conscious decision about what to believe. You told the group, that eventful night at the hospital, that they (we) should also make the decision and believe that God would answer if we asked and believed. Well, I was impressed then, and even today, with your practical demonstration of asking and believing. Thanks for letting me learn from the example you set."

HD Reddin—friend

*****

"I live in a very remote area in Botswana, Africa. I "just happened' to be at a phone in the Village when I received the call about Cody. I immediately phoned the hospital in Houston and was so stirred when I spoke with Ella to find these parents who could have been hysterical—perfectly calm, though tired, but filled with potent faith. Webster's meaning of potent: "having great authority or influence; powerful; might; procreative." That is the kind of faith I heard. I was on my way to our Women's Aglow meeting and afterwards a group of fired-up African women joined our faith, with hundreds and thousands of other believers, for Cody's recovery. What a wonderful testimony this has been to the people here who have heard of God's faithfulness to the Brunt family."

Jana Lackey—Missionary, Botswana, Africa

*****

"I remember the evening my husband called me from church, to say that Cody Brunt had been in a boating accident and had drowned. As he was going on with the conversation, telling me Cody had been resuscitated and taken by Life Flight to the medical center, I honestly never heard a word he was saying beyond the initial news that Cody had drowned. You see, I am a registered nurse and organ transplant coordinator. The reality was that Cody would most likely be an excellent organ donor. I later commented, in the office, that we would probably be having a young donor, soon, from Hermann Hospital. I fully intended to be the one to help Ted and Ella through this decision and that stayed heavy on my mind. As time went by, the news was not encouraging, Cody was ventilator dependent. His oxygen saturation was very near not being compatible with life. One of the criteria to establish brain death, before a person is considered a candidate as an organ donor, is three EEG's demonstrating no brain activity. These were being given and I was expecting to receive a call soon.

Yes, I was expecting Cody to die. My faith was not, at that time, where it should have been concerning healing. One afternoon, a few days after the accident, my husband and I went to visit Cody. I was afraid Ted and Ella would see through my words and actions and know that what I really thought was so negative. That was the day I changed. I grew stronger in my faith and actually repented forever for not completely 100% trusting Jesus to take care of any situation. The thing I had not expected was the faith I saw in Cody's parents. NOT ONE SINGLE NEGATIVE WORD CAME OUT OF EITHER OF THEIR MOUTHS. They spoke only of his healing and coming home. They refused to allow the devil to use the situation to lessen their faith. They quoted scripture in every conversation and looked only to a positive outcome. *I must tell you this changed my life.* After I saw their faith and felt the anointing of God around Cody's bed, I knew he was going to live. Now I take every opportunity I have to tell others that Jesus is our Healer and Cody is a great testimony to Jesus' healing power. Expect a miracle and you will get one!"

Nancy Eisenhour, R.N.—nurse and friend

*****

"The experience of helplessly watching your lifeless son being pulled from the water must reach the greatest level of devastation one can imagine. And watching God's miracle-working power raise your son from the dead—what an awesome God we serve! "<u>God Always Wins</u>" is an amazing story of life, death, and "life after death", with a detailed account of why listening to what God says at the right time can impact eternity. Ella and her family were armed for battle, powerfully fought the one that came to destroy, and lived to jubilantly proclaim God's glory. The spirit of the message in this book will challenge your hearts, question your personal "readiness", and inspire your commitment to our life-giving Lord as you watch Him breathe into Cody's body—for a second time. I encourage you to take advantage of this 1990's account illustrating the healing power of God's touch, when nothing else would do."

Patti Moore—Friend

*****

"When Misty May called me late on the evening of the accident, my heart sank. She told me the hospital staff had just allowed about 19 friends and family members in to see Cody in the PICU unit. I knew that meant only one thing, they were not expecting him to make it through the night. I knew too well policies were relaxed with dying children (or policies were lifted in the case of dying children).

The next day was even harder for me to pray. Knowing hospital procedures, it was only a matter of time before the transplant team would be approaching Ted and Ella about allowing Cody's organs to be donated. First, there must be flat line EEG's. Now, they were on their second one. All that would come from my innermost being was, "Oh God, please!" I have been privileged to witness such a great miracle of life in Cody. Each time I look at him, I am reminded of God's goodness."

Beth Cantini, RN, BSN—Friend and Nurse

*****

"Cody's miracle is a true story of God's healing power. His parents, Ted and Ella, along with Brittany, are true heroes of Faith as well as dear friends."
Tommy and Rachel Burchfield—Burchfield Ministries

*****

"At the time of the accident, I was Cody's care pastor. I well remember arriving at the hospital, to find a family fighting off the grief of the moment, due to the circumstances that were staring them in the face. But praise God, they had other information in this dark situation—that said they could change things totally! I found a family, united and saying what God said. They had been trained for just such a time as this and now…They were "working the Word" of God…That would guarantee them the result they needed. I heard words of faith, flowing powerfully from their lips! They were not considering the hopeless looking situation, but were calling things that were not as though they were! They were taking the guarantees from God's Word and speaking them out through lips of faith. I could immediately tell that this was a family that would not be denied God's promise! God had given them their son and they were keeping him and raising him to serve God. I joined my faith with theirs, for the results, we knew, were coming our way. God gets all of the glory. I praise God for a family who knew the word of God for such a time as this…"
Mike Stanley—Missionary

*****

"Having been friends with Ted and Ella for many years, it is not at all unusual to receive a phone call when you need prayer, agreement, counseling, favors, or to talk. I was in the delivery room when Brittany and Cody were born and our friendship runs deep. This has helped to make Brittany and Cody much more special in my life.

That day, Ella called me on her way to Hermann Hospital, in Houston. I asked how Cody was and she replied, "Well, his heart is beating." I didn't think anything of it and said, "OK, Praise God, keep me posted." Then I made a phone call to my pastor's wife. Cindy said Ella had just called and they were doing CPR on Cody at the time. Being a nurse and knowing the nature of CPR, I was speechless for a second. Ella had not said anything about CPR and she seemed so calm. When I hung up, I immediately picked up my purse and took off for the hospital. Cody was like a son to me. When I got there, several other members of the church began to quickly arrive. The doctor finally came out and asked for family, I volunteered. He began with, "Cody is a very critical child with two major problems right now." The first was the fact that, when he arrived, a Cat Scan had been performed on his head, and he had brain damage, but it was not from trauma to the head. I then asked him if Cody responded to pain.

He said, "No". I then asked if he responded to deep pain, again the answer was "No". (These were also signs of probable, irreversible brain damage or no brain function). I then asked, "Since the brain damage was not from trauma to the head, (like something hitting him on the head), was he trying to say that the damage was from loss of oxygen for an extended period of time?" The answer was "Yes". The doctor said that was not really his most critical problem at the time, but that his major problem was with his lungs. There is so much lung damage and his lungs were literally beginning to deteriorate and bleed, which at this time they were unable to stop. They were going to try high pressures on the ventilator but they may have to resort to experimental drugs. It was a critical time right now. I then asked what was Cody's oxygen level in his blood. By the look on his face, he was surprised with such technical questions. I informed him that I was a nurse and wanted to know. He then told us that Cody's' oxygen level was 40 percent and the desired level was 90-100 percent. The 40 percent registered on 100 percent oxygen on the respirator. The doctor then told us that they would let us know when we could go in to see Cody, but it would be a little while.

Based on my medical knowledge, in my mind, I knew what was really going on, but did not want to say anything to the group. We immediately joined hands and began to pray and confess the Word of God over Cody.

On the drive home that night, the devil immediately began putting thoughts in my mind. Since Ted and Ella were temporarily living in an apartment, I could offer my home as a place for after Cody's funeral…I cast those thoughts down and began to pray like I've never prayed before. I had faith like I never used before to see such a creative miracle. Cody needed a new brain and new lungs.

The following weeks or so went by quickly. I couldn't wait to get off work and drive up to Houston and see the progress. It was exciting to see God's miracle working power on a daily basis with Cody just being alive. As a nurse, I saw and witnessed a true miracle.

I will always look back on and remember how faithful God is to perform His Word."
Misty May—R.N. friend

*****

"While sitting in my office at church waiting for the Wednesday night service to begin, I received a call that Ted and Ella's son, Cody, had drowned in a boating accident in Clear Lake. They had Life Flighted him to Hermann Hospital. I left a message for Pastor Hallam and took off for Houston. I met Misty May there and the doctor came out of PICU and spoke to us about Cody's condition. At that time it was very grim. The doctor gave us the worse case scenario and offered little hope. We started praying while others showed up. Ted asked the doctor if it was okay for all of us to go in and lay our hands on him and pray. The doctor said that at this point anything could help. We went in and crowded around his bed. The first thing I noticed was that big hose going in his throat and that lifeless body hooked up to the machine. Ted looked at me and said, "Brother James, you are the spiritual authority from the church, I want you to lead us in the prayer of agreement with me and his mother for 100 percent recovery spirit, soul, and body. I don't even want him afraid of water!" What the devil tried to use for evil, God would turn around for good. I remember leaving the room with the feeling that the fight was on. Days went by and there was no physical sign of any change, in fact the reports only got worse. (I had been in this fight before with my wife when she had spinal meningitis.) My faith would not let go of what we prayed. For ten days, I came every night, staying till 1:00 and 2:00 in the morning with Ted and Ella, watching the medical staff work on Cody. We would just speak faith statements over Cody. I told Ella to write a journal of everything going down. I told her one day this miracle was going to make a great book or even a movie. It was so easy to be a part of this family of faith.

I grew so much watching them stand so strong. The hospital room was a constant hub of prayer, witnessing and praying for so many others who needed prayer. We prayed for whatever the doctors said they needed to see. Now the second phase of this trial was on. This was the hardest for Ella, to watch him toss, pull, and cry. My wife, Debbie, broke and cried watching her student, who she loved, in this condition. Almost like spiritual doctors, we asked everyday what we needed to pray for to take back to the church and pray corporately over them. To look at him today and see him swimming, playing, and doing great in his studies, gives my life strength and activates my faith to look always to God who truly is the Author and Finisher of our faith."

James Benson—Minister

✶✶✶✶✶

"It is with great love that I write about this "Mighty man of God". I was at the hospital when Cody was born and took my duty as his "Aunt Barb" to put on his first pair of socks. The Lord gave me the scripture to pray over him, found in Ephesians 6:15, *"...having shod your feet with the preparation of the gospel of peace."* Little did we know that later in his life, this prayer would be tested.

I remember sitting in church that Wednesday, on the night of the accident. Fear started to come over me, but the Lord reminded me of the prayer we had prayed over him when he was first born. The next day I went to Hermann hospital and standing at Cody's bedside, the Lord reminded me of those precious socks of "peace" and "protection". The next Sunday afternoon, I brought a pair of socks Pastor Hallam had preached in and placed them on his feet. We again believed God; the scripture would be fulfilled. That was my contribution with prayer to see this little man recover."

Barbara Ward—R.N. and Friend

*****

On the fateful night of Cody's accident, I received a telephone call at my home informing me that an announcement had just been made during the Wednesday night service at my home church that Cody had died in a boating accident and that all of the family was at the hospital. I immediately called the emergency room at the Hermann Hospital in Houston and the receptionist said that she could not give me any information. I asked to be transferred to the room where some member of the family could talk with me. To my surprise, Ella answered the phone. As soon as she knew it was me, she began to say, "Cody will live and declare the works of the Lord" and other strong confessions. She told me that the doctor had just informed them that he would allow the group of family and friends present to go in and see Cody and pray for him. Since I had been told that Cody died, I believed that they were going to go in and pray for Cody to be raised from the dead. I knew of Ella and Ted's strong faith and such a response would be in keeping with what I knew about them. I was stunned. I got off the phone and began to pray. I must confess that I did not have the faith to believe for Cody to be raised from the dead. All I could do was pray for the family.

I work in downtown Houston, and had occasion several times over the next days and weeks to visit Cody and see the family at the hospital on my lunch break. It was truly an amazing thing to witness this couple's "faith in action" in the fact of the most devastation and overwhelming medical reports. Never did I hear anything but the promises of God come out of their mouths. They chose to believe and confess the "Good report" of God's promises. Slowly the true miracle of God came apparent as Cody fully recovered.

Today Cody is a totally well child, whole in every way. What a faithful God we serve!

Judy Robinson—Attorney at Law
Highlands, Texas

Cody Brunt today.

Few people have the privilege of leaving this earth, going to heaven and returning to tell about it. Cody is a living example that God still works miracles today. NOTHING is impossible with God!

Cody with Ted on graduation day with his bachelor degree with honors.
University of Texas at M.D. Anderson Cancer Center—Houston

**Cody with his published mystery novel
(He worked on this project since high school)**

**Current family photo—2014
Cody, Ella, Ted and Brittany**

Cody Brunt is a young man "who is wise beyond his years". At six years old, he drowned in a sail boat accident. The initial doctor's report of "irreversible brain damage" and hemorrhaging lungs were not received by his parents who immediately relied on The Word of God to stand on and demand his 100% recovery. Through a series of miracles, the Lord gave him a new brain and new lungs. The things Cody experienced while he was NOT on this earth have stayed with him. Cody has always had a desire to return to heaven because of the awesome sights of this extraordinary experience. The things that he saw and experienced in heaven impacted his life with a Divine longing to return that has never left him. After all these years, this experience has been inside him, but just recently the time has come for him to share it with the world the joys of heaven and what awaits Christians as their final destination.